May our Lord fills
your life with love

with gratitude
& prayers
Fr. Jean Accoun Helou
2/19/2023

Joel dedicates this book to the following talented friends who have helped to create such amazing art:

David Anderson	**Andy Gregg**	**Matt Lehman**	**Kristi Carter Smith**
Wayne Brezinka	**Aaron Johnson**	**Taaron Parsons**	**Ligia Teodosiu**
Abe Goolsby	**Emily Keafer**	**Edward Patton**	**Darren Welch**
	Michael Korfhage	**Aruna Rangarajan**	

A GRATEFUL ACKNOWLEDGEMENT TO:

My wife, Patty Atlan Anderson: for your love, inspiration, support and partnership for over 28 years.
Dawn Verner: for many hours of research and proofreading while you helped me run the design firm.
Nathan Anderson: for editing and proofreading while giving our fans and customers a taste of Nashville.
Angela Patterson: for researching and writing over 30 great historical sketches for this book.
Beth Odle, Aimee James, Pam Reece & Amber Williams: for helping us find and publish photos from the Downtown Public Library Special Collections Center and the Nashville Room.
Debbie Cox, Leanne Garland & Friends of Metro Archives: for supplying us with historical photos of Nashville.

To purchase classic Music City prints and gifts, please visit:
www.SpiritOfNashville.com

3rd Edition printed, February, 2017
© 2017 Joel Anderson. All rights reserved. Spirit of Nashville is a trademark of Anderson Design Group, Inc.
No portion of this book may be reproduced in any form for any reason without express written consent.

Cover, interior design, and all posters created by Anderson Design Group.
116 29th Avenue North, Nashville, Tennessee 37203. Phone: 615-327-9894. www.ADGstore.com.
All photos used by permission. Printed & produced with pride in Nashville, TN.
Published by Anderson Design Group, Inc.

A Word from the Author...

AS AN ARTIST, I find it much easier to speak with pictures than with words. If a picture is worth a thousand words, then this book really does say a lot about my favorite city in the whole world. I just can't seem to stop creating art that celebrates the history and charm of my adopted hometown. It's a labor of love, bordering on mad obsession. Every time I experience a new Music City moment, I feel compelled to capture the essence of the place, the history, and the stories that made this part of Nashville special to me and so many others.

After living in Dallas, New York, El Salvador, Curaçao, and a few other places, arriving in Nashville was strangely like coming home—as if I had always belonged here. So, in 1986, it was wonderful to begin sending down roots deep in Nashville's rocky, southern soil. Since then, my wife (a Parisian who I married the same year) has come to love Nashville as much as I do. And after living here all these years, we are both proud to call it our home. She became an American citizen here. Our three sons were born here (and our daughter flew to Nashville from Korea to join our family.) Our friends are here, our church is here, our business is here, our best memories are here—so our hearts will always belong here.

Over the years, I have had the privilege of collaborating with fabulously talented people. While working on the Spirit of Nashville Collection, I played the role of a conductor, coaxing beautiful visual melodies from a team of gifted designers and illustrators. I created more than 50 of the posters myself, but almost 100 more were done by my friends who worked under my direction to create this award-winning collection of prints. Without their dedication and cooperation, none of this would have been possible. Since the beginning, twelve different artists have joined forces with me to create over 150 Music City poster designs that all fit together as one cohesive collection.

Combining text with the art was a much bigger job than I could handle alone. So in order to present interesting historical information about the Nashville

icons featured in this book, I called in a professional—someone I met at one of our exhibits who seemed to have an appreciation for the Spirit of Nashville Collection and a fondness for our city. Angela Patterson, a newspaper reporter and journalist, brought her research and writing skills to the rescue. She created over 30 historical sketches to tell the background stories of important landmarks and establishments depicted in many of our poster designs. With the help of the good folks at the Nashville Public Library's Special Collections Center and the Metro Archives, I was able to add beautiful historic photos to Angela's text. Finally, I sprinkled in memories and musings I collected from many people who wanted to express their affection for Nashville. Thanks to all who collaborated with me, this book (much like Music City) is a creative tapestry of art, history, love notes and personal stories.

Many of the places celebrated in our prints are not only historically important to this city, but for sentimental reasons, they are monuments to wonderful moments in Nashville life. And life in Music City just keeps on getting better! Our city consistently ranks among the top places to live in the U.S.A. Our economy is admired as one of the fastest-growing and most diverse in America. People from all over the world choose Nashville over other cities to study, conduct business, vacation or call home.

I'll be the first to admit that the Spirit of Nashville Collection does not cover every aspect of this great city. (I've lived and worked in the West End area, so the art focuses more on my "neck of the woods.") There are still dozens of other worthy landmarks and establishments to feature in future poster designs. Meanwhile, I hope you enjoy exploring Nashville through our art, through the history presented in the text, and through your own memories as you leaf through the pages of this book.

—*Joel Anderson,* Founder of Anderson Design Group & creator of the Spirit of Nashville Collection

---

"The "Spirit of Nashville" series pays tribute to our city's history and growth by showcasing the places we have come to cherish and love in our community. We celebrate this 10th Anniversary Edition and the more than 100 iconic poster designs that promote Nashville, our landmarks, our legends and our culture. These images help preserve our love for Nashville and all it has to offer." —**Karl Dean,** Nashville's mayor 2008-2016

A VISUAL TIMELINE: *200 Years of Nashville History*

1806
Nashville is incorporated as a city on September 11, 1806.

1807
Belle Meade Plantation is founded by John Harding.

1822
The first stone bridge is built across the Cumberland.

1824
Music publishing begins in Nashville with the publication of Western Harmony, a book of hymns and instructions for singing.

1828
Andrew Jackson is elected seventh President of the United States.

1843
Nashville is named the permanent capital of Tennessee.

1845
Construction of the Tennessee State Capitol begins.

1845
Andrew Jackson dies at his home, The Hermitage.

1850
The first steam engine, the No. 1, ordered by the Nashville and Chattanooga Railroad, arrives in Nashville.

1851
The first gas street lamp is lighted at Second Avenue North and the Public Square.

1859
The Tennessee State Capitol is completed.

1862
Federal troops occupy Nashville, the first southern capital to fall to the Union Army.

1863
After 3 days of fighting, the Battle of Stones River ends.

1864
Union troops defeat Confederate forces in the Battle of Nashville, December 15 and 16.

1866
Fisk University founded.

1897
The Centennial Exposition opens with the Parthenon as its centerpiece.

1900
Union Station opens.

1902
Centennial Park is acquired by the city, marking the beginning of Nashville's public park system.

1904
The city's first Carnegie Library opens at the corner of 8th Avenue North and Union Street.

1904
Nashville's first skyscraper is constructed at the southeast corner of Fourth Avenue North and Church Street.

1905
Tennessee State Legislature adopts state flag designed by LeRoy Reeves, April 17th, 1905.

1907
Tony Sudekum opens the first movie theater, The Dixie, on 5th Avenue, North, next to the Arcade.

1910
The Marathon Motor Car is manufactured in Nashville.

1912
The Nashville Reservoir breaks, releasing 25 million gallons of water into the area.

1913
Radnor Lake is constructed by the L&N Railroad.

1916
East Nashville is devastated by fire on March 22, 1916.

1920
The first Nashville Symphony was organized.

1925
Grand Ole Opry begins.

1925
Hillsboro Theatre,

1946
Walter Sharp leads the founding of the Nashville Symphony.

1950
Capitol Records becomes the first major company to locate its director of country music in Nashville.

1951
Belmont College opens.

1957
The L&C Tower is completed.

1957
Cheekwood Botanical Garden & Museum of Art is founded.

1958
The Country Music Association is founded.

1961 The Pancake Pantry opens.

1962
Tennessee's first interstate highway, connecting Nashville to Memphis, arrives in Nashville.

1967
The Barn Dinner Theatre opens.

1967
The Country Music Hall of Fame opens on Music Row, on April 1st, 1967.

1968
Dale Evans and Roy Rogers cohost the CMA Awards.

1970
Percy Priest Lake opens.

1972
Opryland USA opens.

1973
Fox's Donut Den opens.

1990
The Nashville Chamber Orchestra is founded.

1991
Marathon Motor Company Building renovated and used for arts and business space.

1993
Bongo Java opens.

1994
Ryman Auditorium reopens as an entertainment venue June 1st, 1994.

1994
The BellSouth Tower ("the Batman Building") has its grand opening Oct. 20, 1994.

1994
Natchez Trace Parkway Bridge opens on March 22, 1994.

1995
Farmers Market is renovated.

1996
Tennessee Bicentennial Mall State Park opens May 31st. On June 1st, a celebration is held there for our state's 200th birthday.

1996
Frist Center for the Visual Arts named, and plans are drawn up to convert the old U.S. post office building on Broadway into the arts center.

1997
Opryland USA closes with Dec. 31st Christmas in the Park.

1998
April 16th tornado hits downtown Nashville,

damaging homes in East Nashville and blowing down trees at The Hermitage.

1999
Nashville Zoo at Grassmere opens in stages with last animals making the

1867
John Berrien Lindsley founds Montgomery Bell Academy from funds left to the University of Nashville by Montgomery Bell at his death in 1855.

1871
The Jubilee Singers begin a series of singing tours to raise money for the struggling school.

1875
Hatch Show Print opens.

1875
The Fire Alarm Telegraph, with over 20 miles of wire, went into operation.

1873
Vanderbilt University is founded.

1876
Jubilee Hall, the first building in the U.S. constructed for the higher education of African Americans, is built.

1877
The city's first telephone call is made.

1880
Nashville celebrates the centennial year of its founding.

1882
Nashville sees its first electric light.

1885
Nashville's first professional baseball game is played in Athletic Park near the Sulphur Spring Bottom north of downtown.

1891
David Lipscomb College begins as the Nashville Bible School.

1892
The Union Gospel Tabernacle, now Ryman Auditorium, is completed.

1892
Joel Owsley Cheek develops Maxwell House Coffee blend.

1896
The first automobile is driven in Nashville.

---

later renamed the Belcourt, opens.

1926
Ezell's Dairy (Purity Dairies) was founded by Miles Ezell, Sr.

1927
Percy Warner Park, Tennessee's largest municipal park, is established.

1928
Candyland opens on West End Avenue.

1931
The Parthenon reopens in its permanent form.

1937
The present Davidson County Courthouse is completed and opened.

1939
Ellistion Place Soda Shop opens.

1940
Cumberland River freezes enough on January 27th, 1940 that residents can walk across it.

1940
The Belle Meade Theatre opens.

1941
The first Iroquois Steeplechase is run.

1943
The Grand Ole Opry moves to Ryman Auditorium.

1943
Cornelia Fort becomes the first female pilot to die for her country during wartime.

1974
Station Inn opens.

1974
The Grand Ole Opry moves from Ryman Auditorium to Opryland.

1978
Amtrak passenger train service through Nashville ends.

1978
The Nashville Sounds bring professional baseball back to Nashville.

1980
Tennessee Performing Arts Center opens.

1982
The Bluebird Café opens.

1983
January 10th, Riverfront Park opens on Broadway riverfront.

1985
The General Jackson Showboat launches.

1986
Hog Heaven opens.

1986
Union Station reopens as a hotel.

1986
The Nashville Ballet is established.

1987
The Nashville Convention Center and the new airport open.

1987
The Nashville Shakespeare Festival is founded.

1988
The Parthenon reopens after a two-year renovation of the gallery space.

---

move to Grassmere in the fall.

1999
Ninety-year-old Shelby Street Bridge closes to vehicle traffic and reconstruction as a pedestrian bridge begins.

2000
Titans Parade on February 1st for American Football Conference Champion Tennessee Titans after the Super Bowl.

2001
The Frist Center for the Visual Arts opens in what was formerly Nashville's historic main post office on April 8th.

2001
The Country Music Hall of Fame opens at a new downtown location at 222 Fifth Avenue South on May 17th.

2001
The Nashville Public Library opens a new downtown library at 615 Church Street on June 9th, completing a $125 million plan to build the new 315,000 sq. ft. main library and 5 regional branches.

2003
Shelby Street Bridge reopens as a pedestrian bridge linking downtown and East Nashville on August 3.

2004
Gateway Bridge opens as a new link over the Cumberland River on May 19.

2006
Schermerhorn Symphony Center opens with ribbon cutting on September 7 and gala Nashville Symphony performance on September 9.

2006
Public Square dedication on October 1 kicks off "Celebrate Nashville" festivities to mark 200th anniversary of incorporation of the city and election of Nashville's first mayor.

LANDMARKS & *History*

1. Bicentennial Mall
2. Riverfront Park
3. View of skyline & bridges
4. The Parthenon in Centennial Park
5. Cornelia Fort Airpark (former site)
6. Natchez Trace Parkway bridge
7. The Hermitage
8. Belle Meade Plantation
9. Union Station
10. Tennessee State Capitol
11. General Jackson dock
12. Lane Motor Museum
13. Vanderbilt University
14. Fisk University
15. Belmont University
16. Lipscomb University
17. Watkins College of Art, Design & Film
18. Trevecca Nazarene University
19. Hume Fogg High School
20. Anderson Design Group Studio Store
21. Lower Broadway
22. John Seigenthaler Pedestrian Bridge
23. Music City Center

MUSIC & *Melody*

24. Country Music Hall of Fame & Museum
25. Bluebird Cafe
26. Station Inn
27. Nashville Symphony
28. Ryman Auditorium

ARTS & *Leisure*

29. Frist Center for the Visual Arts
30. Cheekwood Botanical Garden & Museum of Art
31. Nashville Ballet
32. Nashville Sounds Stadium
33. Adventure Science Center
34. Hatch Show Print
35. Nashville Zoo
36. Chaffin's Barn Dinner Theatre
37. Belle Meade Theatre Marquee
38. Belcourt Theatre
39. Shakespeare in the Park
40. Percy Priest Lake
41. Radnor Lake
42. Percy Warner Park
43. Iroquois Steeplechase
44. War Memorial Plaza & Auditorium
45. McCabe Golf Course
46. Fort Negley
47. Shelby Park
48. Hadley Park
49. Public Square Park
50. Cumberland Park
51. Bells Bend Park
52. Two Rivers Mansion
53. Fanny Mae Dees (Dragon Park)
54. Nashville Music Garden

FOOD & *Flavor*

55. Loveless Cafe
56. Nashville Farmers Market
57. Purity Dairies
58. Vandyland
59. Fox's Donut Den
60. Pancake Pantry
61. Elliston Place Soda Shop
62. Bongo Java
63. Hog Heaven
64. Arnold's Country Kitchen
65. Bobbie's Dairy Dip
66. Swett's
67. Mére Bulles
68. Mas Tacos
69. The Cupcake Collection
70. Fido
71. The Peanut Shop

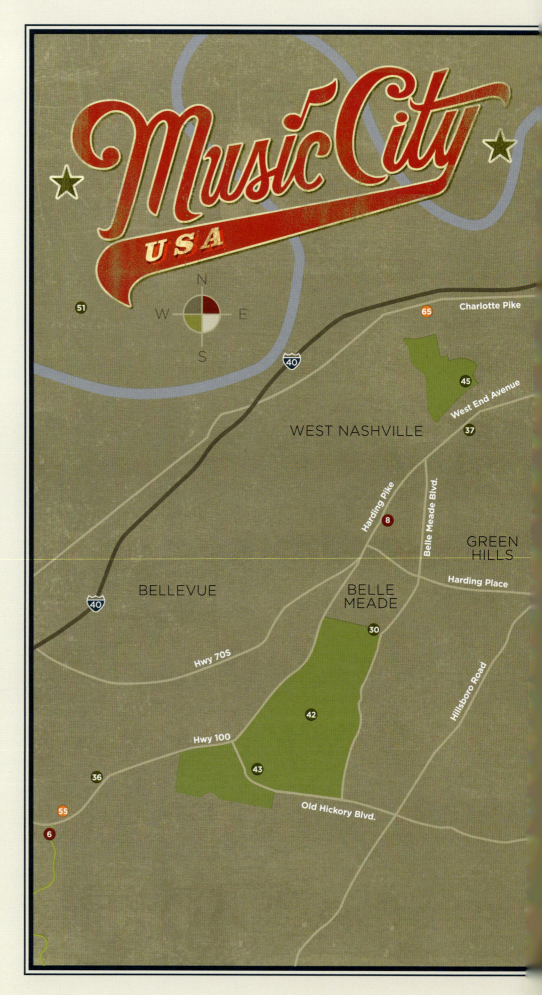

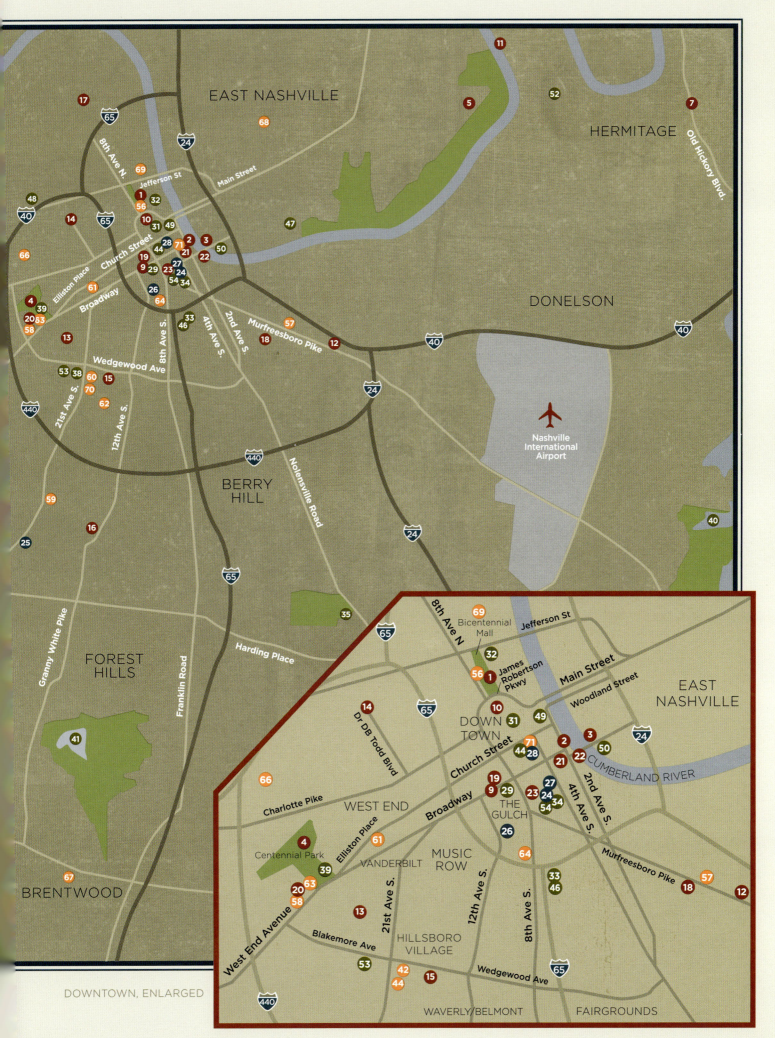

DOWNTOWN, ENLARGED

TENNESSEE'S CAPITAL CITY

THREE STARS punctuate the noonday sky. Set on a crimson banner waving above the Nashville skyline, these converging stars represent the union of East, Middle and West Tennessee. From the Great Smoky Mountains, to the rolling highlands and on to the western plains, three distinct regions of Tennessee are like patches stitched together onto the same quilt. This colorful union is personified by the spirit of Tennessee's capital city. What is the Spirit of Nashville? It is the rich heritage—the flavors, sights, sounds and stories of a vibrant 200-year-old community that has always been at the center of a quiltwork of cultures.

The historic capital of the Volunteer State is home to over a million people, many of whom have moved here from all over the USA to enjoy Nashville's booming economy, diverse culture and southern comfort. People from all walks of life—musicians, athletes, researchers, doctors, business people, educators, artists, clergy and students continue to come together under the state flag, making this middle-Tennessee town one of the most exciting places in the South.

But Nashville wasn't always such a big and bustling city. Originally founded as Fort Nashborough in 1779 by James Robertson, it was renamed in 1784 in honor of Francis Nash, a Revolutionary War soldier, when the fort grew enough to be established as a town. It became the capital of Tennessee in 1843 and has been growing ever since.

Tennessee State flag design by LeRoy Reeves

The Tennessee State Flag is considered by many graphic artists to be one of the best state flag designs in the union. It was designed by LeRoy Reeves, a member of the Third Regiment, Tennessee Infantry. It was officially adopted by the Tennessee State Legislature on April 17, 1905.

The geometric design symbolizes the geographical and cultural heritage of the state of Tennessee while echoing the colors of the national flag of The United States of America. The color white symbolizes purity. The blue symbolizes the love that Tennesseans feel for their state and the red symbolizes, that in times of war and peace, Tennesseans are true-blooded Americans.

Mr. Reeves explained his design: "The three stars are of pure white, representing the three grand divisions of the state. They are bound together by the endless circle of the blue field, the symbol being three bound together in one—an indissoluble trinity. The large field is crimson. The final blue bar relieves the sameness of the crimson field and prevents the flag from showing too much crimson when hanging limp. The white edgings contrast more strongly the other colors."

> "When my parents announced, right before I started my junior year of high school, that we would be moving to Nashville from our home of 12 years outside Philadelphia, I thought my life was over. It was a difficult year for the whole family—switching schools, jobs, houses, neighborhoods—and let's face it—cultures! The move was five years ago and now, looking at the list of places featured in this book, I couldn't possibly pick just one to talk about: Bongo Java was where I had lunch with my mom and sister one day while looking at houses before we moved, and it became the place where my fiance and I would meet every time he came through town; Vanderbilt is what brought us here in the first place for my father's job at the Children's Hospital; I've experienced some of the most awe-inspiring music from the lips and fingers of friends and strangers alike at the Bluebird Cafe, Station Inn and the Ryman; I saw foreign films at the Belcourt Theatre with my new high school friends; and I spent many a beautiful Southern summer day in Centennial Park by the Parthenon. I still sometimes stutter when people ask me where I'm from, not knowing which side of the Mason/Dixon line to claim, but when I see the Nashville skyline, I know I can say I am home." — *Emily Baldwin*

< STATE FLAG SKYLINE   18" x 24" Limited Edition Print created in 2003 by Joel Anderson

"This image was on the front of the first Spirit of Nashville calendar which included 14 full-size posters of Music City landmarks. Since Nashville is the capital of Tennessee, it made sense to create an iconic image that set the Nashville skyline on top of our state flag. This design has been one of our most popular prints—even before it was selected to be a permanent fixture on the set of the network TV show Nashville. (Look for it on the wall in scenes that take place in the mayor's office!)"

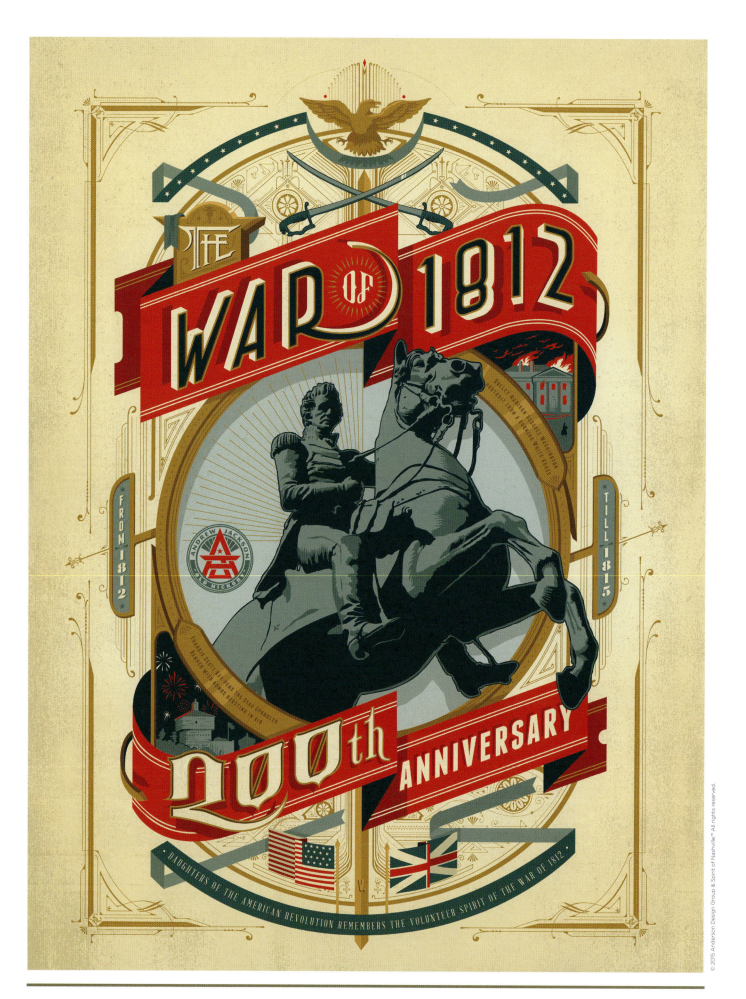

THE WAR OF 1812 (200th ANNIVERSARY PRINT)   18" x 24" Limited Edition Print created in 2012 by Andy Gregg

The War of 1812 was a defining period in the early history of Tennessee. On January 8, 1815, on a battlefield at Chalmette just below New Orleans, Andrew Jackson lead his troops to a shocking American victory in the final and pivotal battle of the War of 1812, ending the three-year war with Britain. General Jackson defeated a British invasion on American soil even though his ragtag army of 4,000 was outnumbered by 10,000 British. This victory forever solidified Andrew Jackson as an American military hero and laid the foundation for his eventual election to the presidency.

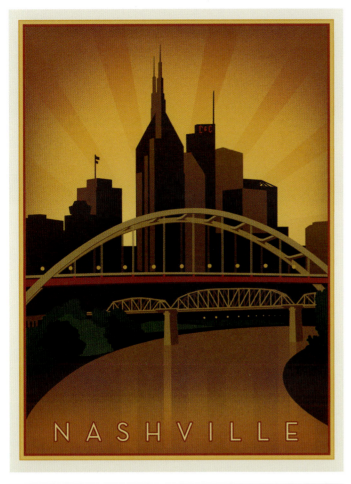
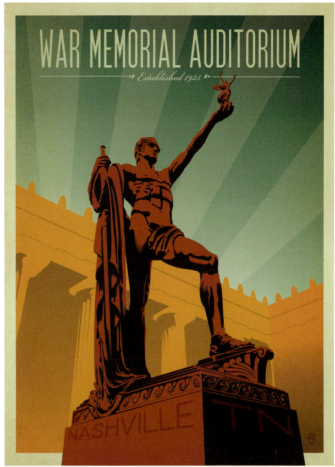

LEGACY BRIDGES OF NASHVILLE   18" x 24" Limited Edition Print created in 2005 by Joel Anderson
WAR MEMORIAL AUDITORIUM   18" x 24" Limited Edition Print created in 2011 by Andy Gregg
GIRL SCOUTS OF MIDDLE TENNESSEE (100 YEAR ANNIVERSARY)   18" x 24" Limited Edition Print created in 2011 by Ligia Teodosiu
NASHVILLE SKYLINE AT NIGHT   18" x 24" Limited Edition Print created in 2004 by Joel Anderson

RIVERFRONT

NASHVILLE'S SKYLINE is punctuated by a stunning 29 story glass structure which towers over the glittering SoBro riverfront district. Located across the street from the Schemerhorn Symphony Center, this mirrored landmark reflects the changing colors of the sky, causing it to appear differently every time you see it. The Pinnacle at Symphony Place was opened in 2010 and is now home to a vital Nashville institution which began operations in October 2000. Pinnacle Financial Partners has since grown to become one of the largest bank holding companies headquartered in Tennessee, providing a full range of banking, investment, trust, mortgage and insurance products. Pinnacle is very supportive in the local community, encouraging associates to volunteer and teach, to help build affordable housing, to promote and encourage the arts, and to beautify the communities they serve.

Pinnacle's majestic glass tower overlooks the historic John Seigenthaler Pedestrian Bridge which crosses over the Cumberland River. This bridge has been given several names over the years. Most recently known as the Shelby Street Pedestrian Bridge, it was originally called the Sparkman Street Bridge when it was completed in 1909. In recent years, it was converted into a walking bridge linking Downtown and East Nashville.

It has become a nighttime icon for the city with its brightly lit girders shining against the evening sky. Designers of the renovation project enhanced the original structure with art elements integrated into the railings at bridge overlooks and added other design features such as wood pavers and stained concrete patterns in the walkway. The Shelby Street Pedestrian Bridge is on the National Register of Historic Places for its significance as one of Nashville's best examples of modern technology and engineering at the turn of the century. It also happens to be one of the best spots in Nashville to enjoy the sparkle of the downtown skyline reflecting off of the Pinnacle at Symphony Place.

Postcard of the Sparkman Street Bridge circa early 1900s.

> "Once upon a time, I met a man on the Shelby Street Bridge. It was the middle of January, bitterly cold, and we were decorating the bridge for a birthday party. From that moment on, I knew this man would either break my heart or I would marry him. Two weeks later, he brought me back for our first kiss. Nine months later, he brought me back and proposed. Four months after that, we walked down the aisle and now we are living happily ever after!" — **Holly Biggs**

< PINNACLE BANK BUILDING ON THE RIVERFRONT   18" x 24" Limited Edition Print created in 2014 by Aaron Johnson

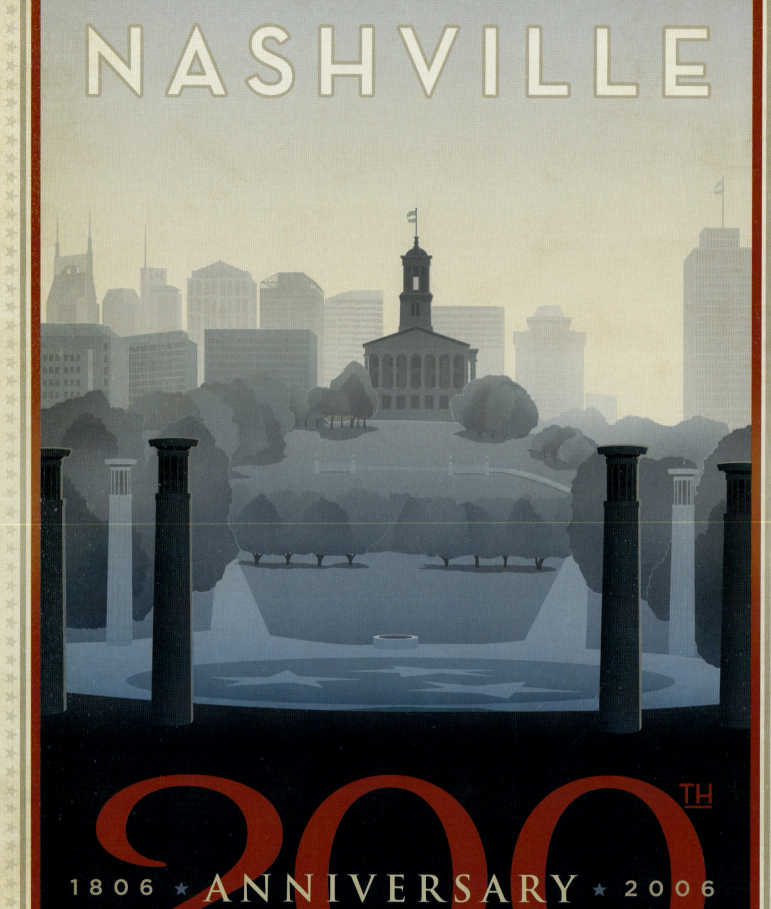

BICENTENNIAL CAPITOL MALL

NO ONE EXPECTS TO SEE an expanse of green grass on the edge of downtown Nashville.

But the Tennessee Bicentennial Capitol Mall State Park offers a majestic view of the state capitol building, and a lovely expanse of green space full of monuments to commemorate the state.

Although thousands of residents and visitors enjoy the park-like environment every year, the original suggestion was to use the space for a large sports stadium. New York urban planning firm Clarke, Rapuano and Holleran thought it would be the ideal use for the large, barren space between James Robertson Parkway and Jefferson Street.

But it was the idea of Knoxville architect Robert Church that would lay the foundation for the Tennessee Bicentennial Capitol Mall, a 19 acre urban park that's the focal point of the Capitol Area master plan.

While his 1969 proposal to create a grand parking structure was rejected, Church's thought to extend the green space and connect the previously detached urban areas would be integrated. Years would pass as more architects would study the land and make recommendations, trying to balance aesthetics with an existing railway path and need for more state office space. But 20 years later, Aladdin Industries employee John Bridges' detailed concept for a mall intrigued both Governor McWherter and Jim Hall, who was charged with directing the state's bicentennial celebration. It was Bridges' concept that would establish the creation of the mall with the historic event.

In 1991, Jerry Preston, assistant commissioner of the Department of Finance and Administration, called together a group of professors and planning professionals to devise a concrete plan for the mall. After reviewing past concepts and assessing present conditions, they created a plan the state accepted, and had a June 1, 1996 deadline, less than five years, in which to execute the project.

Ground was broken on the Mall June 27, 1994. The amphitheater was first constructed; the Mall itself was soon to follow. The many contractors had to work closely together through numerous obstacles, namely a complex construction plan and the watchful eye of CSX railroad officials.

In the end, the park would stretch from the base of Capitol Hill to James Robertson Parkway, where Tennessee Plaza features a fully accurate state map composed of granite. A new railroad trestle serves as the gateway to the Mall,

The 95-bell carillon representing Tennessee's 95 counties.

which includes the Walkway of the Counties, the Riverwall, etc. The ending feature of the Mall is the Court of Three Stars, near Jefferson Street, representing the state's musical heritage.

Although the park was not open, the simultaneous lowering of 95 time capsules—representing the state's 95 counties—on April 27 was the event that marked the Mall as the state's park. The Mall was completed hours before deadline, opening to the public at 8 a.m. May 31, 1996.

The amphitheater lies in front of the train trestle and a majestic view of the State Capitol.

< BICENTENNIAL CAPITOL MALL 18" x 24" Limited Edition Print created in 2006 by Joel Anderson

"When illustrating this view of the Bicentennial Mall with the majestic State Capitol and the downtown skyline set as a backdrop, I had to climb to the top of a building that faced the Mall. Even then, the vantage point was not high enough to make the State Capitol building stand above the skyline. To create a pleasing composition, a little artistic license was required. If you stand across the street from the Mall and look toward the Capitol, you will notice a few of the liberties I took to elevate the Capitol and squeeze the buildings closer together."

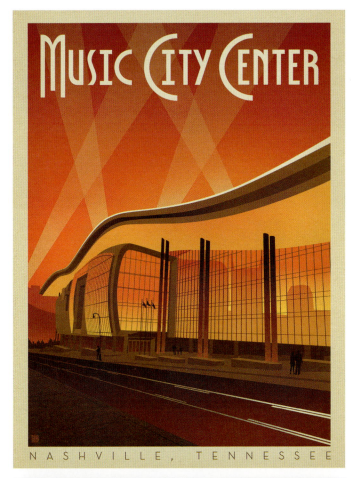

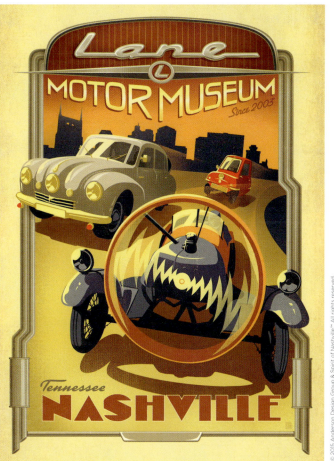

< NASHVILLE SKYLINE (HORIZONTAL) 24" x 18" Limited Edition Print created in 2012 by Michael Korfhage & Joel Anderson
< SHELBY STREET PEDESTRIAN BRIDGE 24" x 18" Limited Edition Print created in 2014 by Michael Korfhage & Joel Anderson
MUSIC CITY CENTER 18" x 24" Limited Edition Print created in 2013 by Michael Korfhage & Joel Anderson
ADVENTURE SCIENCE CENTER 18" x 24" Limited Edition Print created in 2010 by Joel Anderson
WPLN NASHVILLE PUBLIC RADIO 18" x 24" Limited Edition Print created in 2010 by Joel Anderson
LANE MOTOR MUSEUM 18" x 24" Limited Edition Print created in 2013 by Aaron Johnson

THE PARTHENON

A PIECE OF GREECE sits in a park in Nashville. To walk around it is a surreal experience, knowing that the grand columns and the detailed relief sculptures are almost exact replicas of the original Parthenon, and that what you see in front of you is the only full-scale replica of the world-famous building. Technically, it's the only remaining piece of Tennessee's ornate Centennial Celebration in 1896. But the building's stature and prominence also represent the city's one-time image as the "Athens of the South".

In 1893, Colonel W. C. Smith dreamed up the idea of a Centennial Exposition in the hopes it would stimulate both the economy and Nashvillians' interest in their own city. Exposition Director E.C. Lewis would submit a plan in 1895 that included a reproduction of the Parthenon. To ensure the replica would be exact, Lewis requested the drawings and architectural studies from King George I of Greece.

A resolution was adopted by Exposition organizers in 1894 to convert the Parthenon into a fine arts building after the exposition. Over the years, the building deteriorated badly, and patching the exterior-grade plaster was no longer enough. The city's parks board and architect Russell Hart set out to rebuild the structure in 1920. The exterior was completed in 1925, the interior in 1931. The replica was very close to being exact, but lacked one element: a statue of the goddess Athena. Creating such a statue had been discussed for decades, but the Parthenon remained without its goddess until the early 1980s when Alan LeQuire was commissioned to sculpt her. More than seven years later, in May 1990, a 12-ton, 41-feet-10-inch tall statue of Athena was finally unveiled to the public.

Today, the Parthenon remains as impressive as when it was first built. Featuring the largest set of matching bronze doors in the world (weighing 7.5 tons each,) this colossal monument not only welcomes visitors from around the world, but remains the focal point of Centennial Park, one of Nashville's most beautiful and historic public gathering places.

Program for the Centennial Exposition

The Parthenon was originally one of many replicas of exotic architecture at the 1897 Tennessee Centennial Exposition.

< THE PARTHENON 18" x 24" Limited Edition Print created in 2012 by Ligia Teodosiu

"The Parthenon is only two blocks away from the Anderson Design Group studio where all of the Spirit of Nashville posters were created. This print was the 6th in a series of designs requested by Metro Parks to commemorate Nashville's favorite outdoor spaces. The design shows what the park looks like today—without the Egyptian pyramid and other temporary structures shown in the 1897 photo above."

CORNELIA FORT

AT THE TWILIGHT'S LAST GLEAMING

(Excerpts of an article written by Cornelia Fort, just a short time before she was killed in a midair collision over Texas, March 21, 1943. Reproduced from Women's Home Companion, *June 1943.)*

I KNEW I was going to join the Women's Auxiliary Ferrying Squadron before the organization was a reality, before it had a name, before it was anything but a radical idea in the minds of a few men who believed that women could fly airplanes. But I never knew it so surely as I did in Honolulu on December 7, 1941.

At dawn that morning I drove from Waikiki to the John Rodgers Civilian Airport right next to Pearl Harbor, where I was a civilian pilot instructor. Shortly after six-thirty I began landing and take-off practice with my regular student. Coming in just before the last landing, I looked casually around and saw a military plane coming directly toward me. I jerked the controls away from my student and jammed the throttle wide open to pull above the oncoming plane. He passed so close under us that our celluloid windows rattled violently and I looked down to see what kind of plane it was.

The painted red balls on the tops of the wings shone brightly in the sun. I looked again with complete and utter disbelief. Honolulu was familiar with the emblem of the Rising Sun on passenger ships, but not on airplanes.

I looked quickly at Pearl Harbor and my spine tingled when I saw billowing black smoke. Still, I thought hollowly, it might be some kind of coincidence or maneuvers, it might be, it must be. For surely, dear God...

Then I looked way up and saw the formations of silver bombers riding in. Something detached itself from an airplane and came glistening down. My eyes followed it down, down, and even with knowledge pounding in my mind, my heart turned convulsively when the bomb exploded in the middle of the harbor. I knew the air was not the place for my little baby airplane and I set about landing as quickly as ever I could. A few seconds later a shadow passed over me and simultaneously bullets spattered all around me.

Suddenly that little wedge of sky above Hickam Field and Pearl Harbor was the busiest, fullest piece of sky I ever saw.

We counted anxiously as our little civilian planes came flying home to roost. Two never came back. They were washed ashore weeks later on the windward side of the island, bullet riddled. Not a pretty way for the brave yellow Cubs and their pilots to go down to death.

When I returned, the only way I could fly at all was to instruct Civilian Pilot Training programs. Weeks passed. Then, out of the blue, came a telegram from the War Department announcing the organization of the WAFS (Women's Auxiliary Ferrying Squadron) and the order to report within twenty-four hours if interested. I left at once.

Because there were and are so many disbelievers in women pilots, especially in their place in the army, officials wanted the best possible qualifications to go with the first experimental group. All of us realized what a spot we were on. We had to deliver the goods or else. Or else there wouldn't ever be another chance for women pilots in any part of the service.

For all the girls in the WAFS, I think the most concrete moment of happiness came at our first review. Suddenly, and for the first time, we felt a part of something larger. Because of our uniforms which we had earned, we were marching with the men, marching with all the freedom-loving people in the world.

I, for one, am profoundly grateful that my one talent, my only knowledge, flying, happens to be of use to my country when it is needed. That's all the luck I ever hope to have.

Cornelia and the WAFS posing for photos.

Photos courtesy of the Friends of Metro Archives and Nashville Public Library, The Nashville Room

---

< CORNELIA FORT 18" x 24" Limited Edition Print created in 2005 by Darren Welch

"This poster was created to celebrate Cornelia Fort, the first female pilot in American history to die for her country. Fort was a pilot and flight instructor in WWII and was one of the few airborne witnesses to the attack on Pearl Harbor. Cornelia flew all sorts of planes, transporting them to and from various air bases. (This poster features a P-51 Mustang fighter plane.) Fort's achievements are commemorated by an airpark named in her honor."

NATCHEZ TRACE PARKWAY

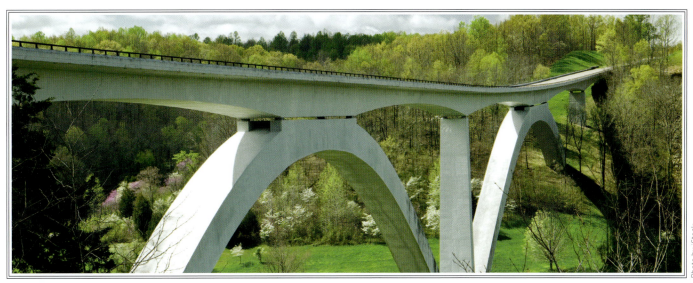

The 444-mile Natchez Trace Parkway commemorates an ancient trail that connected southern portions of the Mississippi River to central Tennessee. Today, visitors can experience this beautiful stretch of road through hiking, biking, horseback riding and camping.

IT'S AN UNEXPECTED SIGHT. Just a few short miles along the 444-mile Natchez Trace parkway, a sleek, white bridge appears, spanning the lush valley below.

The bridge is one of the first interest points along the Trace when traveling from Nashville. It has become a favorite subject for photographers and sightseers, who come from all across the country to travel the historic Natchez Trace.

The Trace itself first appeared as a Native American trade route between area tribes, and was further developed in the early 1800s as a postal route. Eventually, the trail became suitable for travel and trade between the ports of Louisiana, and the North. Settlements sprang up along its path, and many differing people—from circuit preachers to highway bandits —could be found passing from town to town.

It was the introduction of the steamboat to the Mississippi River that eventually rendered the Natchez Trace obsolete; it was abandoned as an official road in 1830. However, just 100 years later, the government saw fit to commemorate the Trace by beginning construction on the Natchez Trace Parkway, which closely follows the original path of the Trace.

The Natchez Trace Parkway Bridge is the crowning jewel of the scenic roadway. Completed in 1994, its creation made engineering history. Designed by Figg Engineering Group and built by PCL Civil Constructors, Inc., the 1,648-foot-long bridge was the first in America to use precast segmented technology for an arched structure. Because of the design, the bridge has won 16 design awards, including prizes from National Endowment for the Arts, the Presidential Award for Design Excellence, and the Eleventh Annual Bridge Conference, which named it the single most outstanding achievement in the bridge industry for 1994.

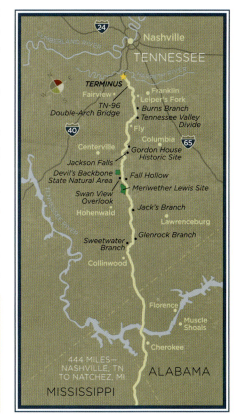

> "What a great place to get away from the city lights and watch the stars. My dad has recently taken up astronomy and he and I took his telescope out there this past Thanksgiving. I saw Saturn through the scope with my very own eyes—it really does have rings!" — **Rachel Paul**

< NATCHEZ TRACE PARKWAY 18" x 24" Limited Edition Print created in 2003 by Kristi Carter Smith

"The bridge is overwhelming in person—trying to capture it in a poster design just doesn't do it justice. You really have to see it in person to appreciate the scale and beauty of this bridge. And if you are not afraid of heights, be sure to walk across the bridge and look over the rail—the views of Birdsong Hollow below are stunning."

THE HERMITAGE

NASHVILLE, TENNESSEE

HOME OF

Andrew Jackson

7TH U.S. PRESIDENT, HERO OF THE WAR OF 1812, ETC.

THE HERMITAGE

EACH YEAR, both tourists and locals file in and out of The Hermitage, the stately Greek Revival-style monument of famed Tennessean Andrew Jackson. People walk through the home that looks much like it did at the end of Jackson's second presidency, viewing his sword collection, library, and collection of family photos.

And while it may be a tourist attraction today, to Andrew Jackson, The Hermitage was much more than just the mansion—it was his refuge from the trials and frustrations of public life. Jackson's wife, Rachel, chose the site for the home and it was subsequently built in 1819 to her specifications. Jackson also commissioned a garden for Rachel; each day she brought fresh flowers from her beloved garden to decorate or to give to visitors.

By the time The Hermitage was built, Andrew Jackson was already an American historical figure. After helping to write the Tennessee constitution in 1796, Jackson was elected the Volunteer State's first congressman, serving a year in the House of Representatives and a year in the U.S. Senate. He later served as judge of the superior court in Tennessee, was elected major general of the Tennessee militia, and won national fame in 1815 with his amazing victory over the British in New Orleans. In 1821, he was appointed governor of Florida, paving his way to a run for the presidency.

Andrew Jackson took office as the seventh president of the United States in 1829. Although he was busy fulfilling duties, he kept close eye on his Tennessee home. After a chimney fire seriously damaged the mansion in October of 1834, President Jackson hired noted Nashville architects and builders Joseph Reiff and William C. Hume to rebuild the mansion. He also had a Grecian-style "temple and monument" built for Rachel, who died in 1828.

In 1837, Jackson retired from the U.S. presidency and returned to The Hermitage. He died on June 8, 1845 and was laid to rest two days later in a tomb next to his wife Rachel. The State of Tennessee purchased the property from the Jackson family in 1855, and since 1889, the Ladies' Hermitage Association has cared for the property as a historic site on behalf of the State of Tennessee. Thanks to the Association's efforts, almost all of the mansion's contents are original. In 1960, the federal government recognized The Hermitage as a National Historic Landmark. Today, The Hermitage is a 1,120-acre property with museum, recreational and farming activities.

< THE HERMITAGE 18" x 24" Limited Edition Print created in 2004 by Abe Goolsby

"We decided to render this poster in a graphical style, simplifying details and the color palette. While this print turned out very nicely, in hindsight, this poster would have been a good one to attempt in the same pen and ink rendering style that I used to create the Union Station, State Capitol and the Belle Meade Plantation prints."

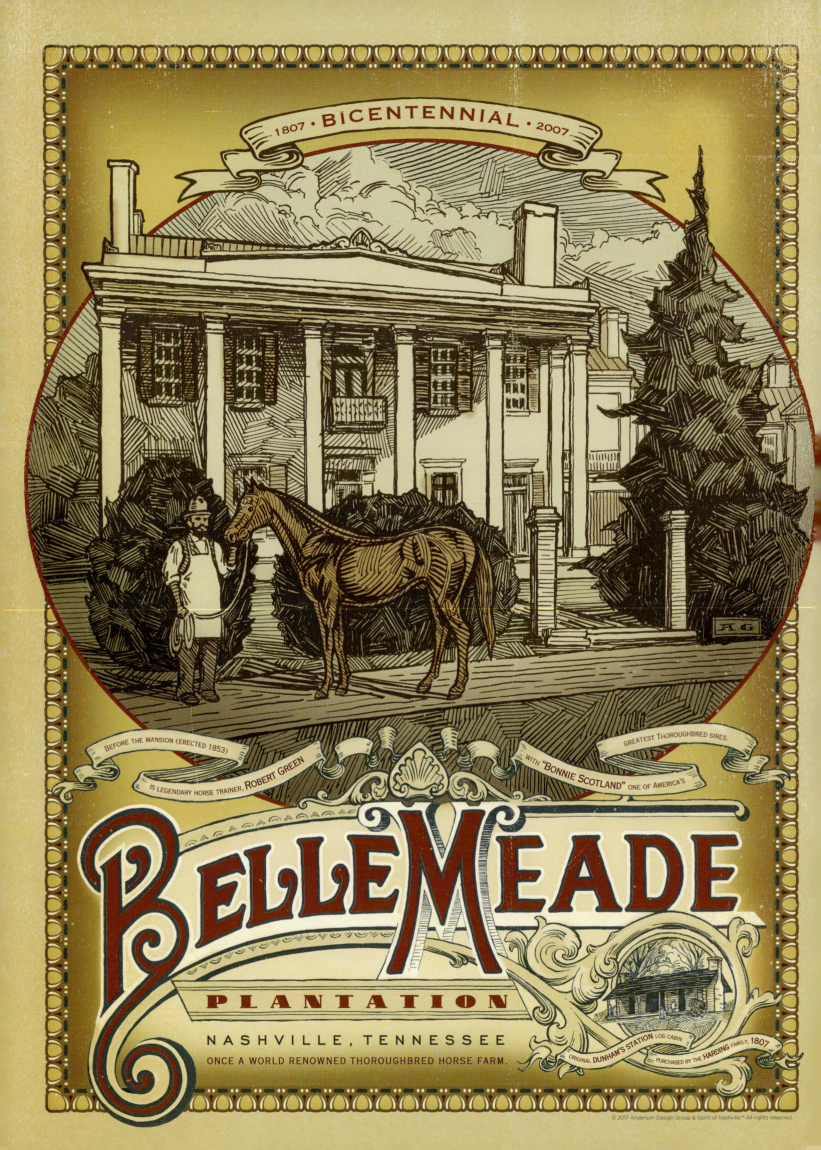

BELLE MEADE PLANTATION

ON A 30-ACRE TRACT of land six miles west of Nashville, it's still 1853.

Among Magnolia trees and stretches of green grass, there's a mausoleum, slave cabin, gardens and stables all surrounding a massive Greek Revival-style mansion.

And each year, visitors flock to Belle Meade Plantation to see this piece of Tennessee history frozen in time.

But what visitors see now is the plantation after 200 years of existence. When John Harding bought the 250-acre tract on the Natchez Trace, he and his wife, Susannah, lived in a small log cabin. The land was cleared, and with the help of slaves, Harding created a farm.

By 1816, the farm sprawled across 1,000 acres and had become a boarding house for thoroughbred horses. As the popularity of horse racing grew, and the farming operation prospered, Harding was able to build a Federal-style brick home for his family. He named his farm Belle Meade, or beautiful meadow.

Harding had been breeding horses at the farm, thanks to Montgomery Bell's stallion Boaster, but it was Harding's son, General William Giles Harding, that would establish the plantation as a well-known breeding facility. Years later, it would be common knowledge that race horse greats such as Secretariat could trace their bloodlines back to Belle Meade. Much of the success is owed to Bob Green, a former slave and expert horse trainer, who worked at the farm his entire life. (He stayed on at the plantation after the Civil War as a freed man.)

Belle Meade thrived before the Civil War, and by the early 1860s, the farm spanned 5,400 acres. General Harding was a Confederate supporter, giving $500,000 to support the Southern cause. But after Nashville surrendered to Union forces in 1862, military governor Andrew Johnson had Harding arrested, and he was sent to Mackinaw Island in Michigan for six months. General Harding's wife Elizabeth handled affairs while he was jailed.

Harding had a stroke in 1883, and turned the farm over to his daughter Selene and her husband, William Hicks Jackson, a retired confederate general who'd commanded troops under General Lee. They managed the farm together, and the farm gained national attention with Jackson's purchase of Iroquois, the first American winner of the English Derby. Iroquois stood stud at Belle Meade Plantation for several years and by the mid 1890s was commanding fees of $2,500 when the average stud fee of the time was $300.00.

After Selene and Billy passed away, the farm was managed by their children. They were ill equipped to operate the estate and after some personal tragedies, the plantation was put up for sale in 1906. The farm was subdivided and passed through the hands of several well-known Nashvillians until 1953 when the mansion and 25 acres of land was purchased by the State of Tennessee. Today, the 30-acre property includes the 1853 mansion and eight other outbuildings, and is operated by the Nashville Chapter of the Association for the Preservation of Tennessee Antiquities. The nonprofit organization is dedicated to the conservation and preservation of the property.

The front of the mansion as it looked around 1900.

The back of the mansion and stables as seen from the surrounding pastures.

< BELLE MEADE PLANTATION 18" x 24" Limited Edition Print created in 2006 by Abe Goolsby

"In the same vein as the Union Station poster, this one was inspired by nineteenth century advertising, with a nod toward the illustrative work of Franklin Booth in the early twentieth century. I took my own reference photography, but also researched and relied on older photographs and paintings, including, of course, the one of Bob Green and Bonnie Scotland which still hangs in the mansion's main foyer."

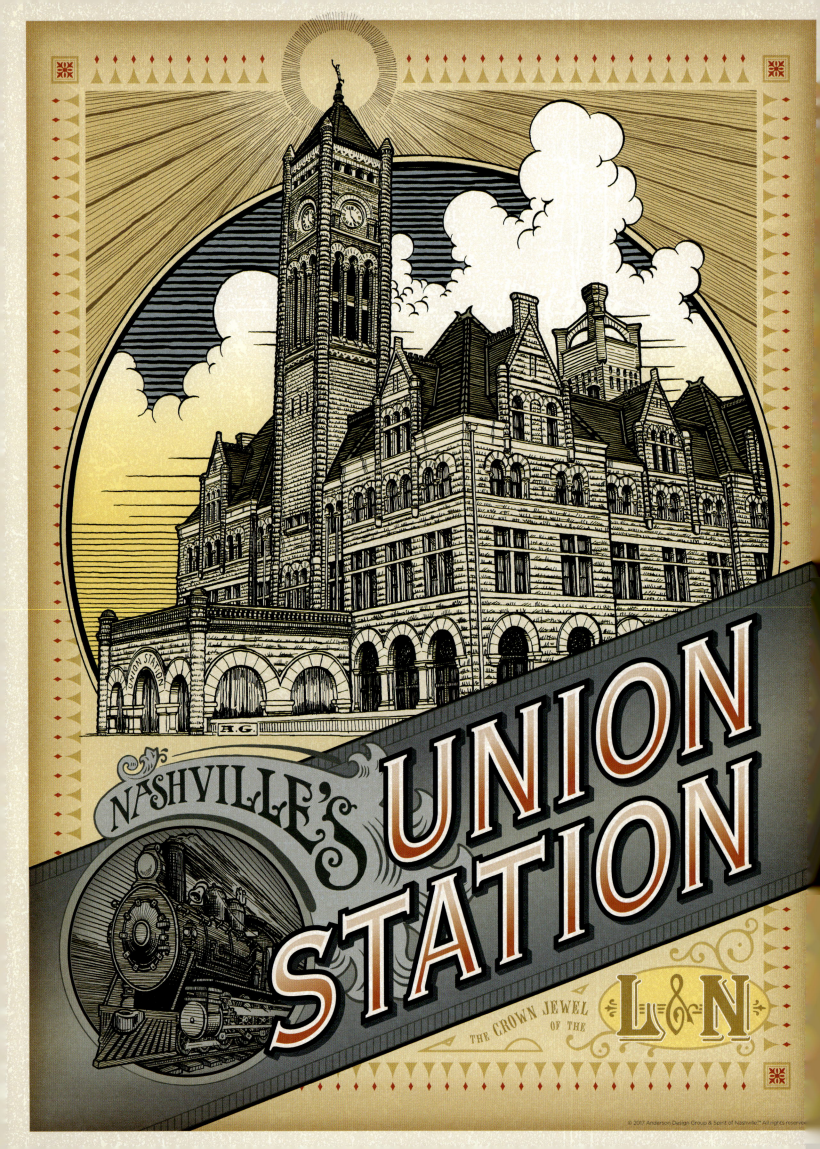

UNION STATION

UNION STATION was opened on October 9, 1900, by the Louisville and Nashville (L&N) and the Nashville, Chattanooga, and St. Louis (NC&StL) Railroads. Made of Kentucky limestone and Tennessee marble, the entire structure was built for $300,000.

Even to this day, most people would describe it as magnificent. To walk in Union Station is to enter a different era, one when travel was a glamorous event, and people put on their best clothing to come to the place that looked like a castle, marveling at the use of Italian marble, vaulted ceilings and stained glass so beautiful it seemed to glow.

And when it was built in 1900, Nashvillians were in awe. Major Eugene C. Lewis, a civil engineer for the NC&StL, was the force behind the building project. A majority of the interest in the NC&StL had been purchased by the L & N Railroad after the Civil War, and therefore they'd be ones financing the project. L&N engineer Richard Montfort designed the structure, and ground was broken on August 1, 1898. More than 200,000 cubic yards of ground were dug up and hauled off in wagons. As masons worked, adding stone after as each floor was built, the Romanesque-style building began to take shape. While pointed gables lined the top of the building, two towers rose above the roof line; the front one was topped with a statue of Mercury, which Lewis had kept from the state's Centennial Exposition.

On October 9, 1900, all of Nashville gathered along Broad Street for the parade and opening, which was more than just an event—it was the town's transition into the new century. The passenger train shed, which measured 250 by 500 feet, was quite the engineering feat in its time—it could hold up to 10 trains at once.

Over the next 70 years, countless amounts of people would file through the station: some to travel, some to eat at the famed restaurant, others just to watch, hoping they might catch a glimpse of a star like Mae West (who did once travel through the station) walking through. In 1977, the station was condemned. The city purchased the quickly declining structure in 1985. By 1986, the station was restored to its original grandeur and reborn as a hotel and restaurant.

Today, Union Station is still a Nashville landmark, attracting travelers and serving as the site for a number of weddings and other events. But the emotions the building evokes have not changed. As Dr. Kate Zerfoss said in one of the many books on the station:

"There was just a majesty about the building; you never felt as you went in and out of it that you hadn't had a lofty feeling by having viewed such a magnificent interior."

< UNION STATION   18" x 24" Limited Edition Print created in 2003 by Abe Goolsby

"This print was created by combining hand lettering with painstakingly detailed pen and ink drawings. I took reference photography, then did perspective drawings in pencil, and finally drew each tile, stone and window pane with a pen and ink. The inspiration for the lettering styles and colors came from old advertising art from the late nineteenth century. I've always been a train fanatic. As a child of four or five years, I boarded what was probably one of the last passenger trains to leave the Station, back in the twilight of its service as an actual railroad depot – a very fond memory."

TENNESSEE STATE CAPITOL

The State Capitol dominated the Nashville skyline in the early 1900s.

The House of Representatives Chamber is as grand as the exterior.

THE MAJESTIC Tennessee State Capitol stands proudly on a hill overlooking downtown Nashville. Upon its completion in 1859, it was considered one of the most magnificent public buildings of its time anywhere in the United States. The cornerstone of the State Capitol was laid on July 4, 1845, and the final stone was put in place on July 21, 1855, more than ten years later.

The architect, William Strickland, designed the distinctive tower after the monument of Lysicrates in Athens, Greece. The building is considered by many to be the masterpiece of Strickland's career, which began with his apprenticeship to Benjamin Latrobe, first architect of the U.S. Capitol. Strickland moved to Nashville from Philadelphia, believing that his stay would be only a few years. Instead, the construction of the Capitol took more than 9 years to complete.

Construction was often delayed because of a shortage of funds. To make matters worse, Strickland had to deal with a man named Samuel Morgan, who was appointed by the Capitol Commission to oversee Strickland's work and make sure that it came in under budget. Legend has it that the two men hated one another and never agreed on anything, getting into heated arguments at the construction site, bickering over details such as cost, materials, and design.

In 1854, William Strickland died, long before the project was complete. In his memory, and according to his wishes, the state voted to construct a vault within the building's walls where his body would be interred. In its entire history, Tennessee has only honored one other man in such a manner; his name was Samuel Morgan!

Some believe even after the two men were interred within the walls of the Capitol, Strickland and Morgan have never stopping arguing. Over the years, police officers have reported strange night-time disturbances at the Capitol, hearing sounds of two men yelling and cursing, but upon investigation, finding the area completely vacant. Some Nashvillians go as far as to say that the Capitol is haunted.

Today, the Capitol is still in use by the state government. It features numerous works of art, historical murals and frescos, portraits, massive chandeliers, as well as the House and Senate chambers, library, and the Governor's Office. It is one of the oldest and most beautiful structures in downtown Nashville, and is open to the public at no charge—but only during the daytime!

< TENNESSEE STATE CAPITOL 18" x 24" Limited Edition Print created in 2004 by Abe Goolsby

"I took reference photography from the top of a nearby office building in an attempt to gain the right vantage point of the Capitol for this design. A few days later, we were surprised to have a pair of plain-clothed agents, apparently from some Bureau of Investigation or other, show up at our studio asking for a certain Abe Goolsby, who had been seen taking surveillance photos of a government building. After a very interesting conversation that lasted maybe fifteen minutes, I was finally able to convince the agents that I was not a terrorist, and merely an artist who was trying to create a nice poster that featured our State Capitol."

HOW THE ART WAS CREATED

State Capitol 18" x 24" pen and ink by Abe Goolsby

1 To begin his poster design, artist Abe Goolsby chose a style that was typical for the late 1850s, the era in which the Tennessee State Capitol was completed. He found examples of the kind of elaborate lettering, borders and line art he wanted to emulate on old tobacco tins. The ornate hand-lettering rendered artfully with curves and embellishments would go perfectly with a detailed pen and ink drawing of the majestic building.

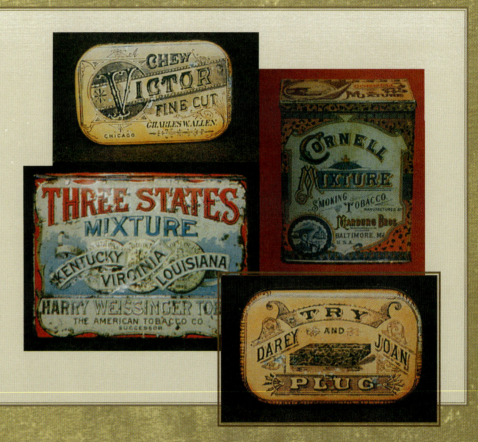

2 The next step was to gather some photographic reference of the State Capitol to aide in creating a pencil drawing that would be inked over to create the poster art of the building. Abe did some library research of archival photos, but the angle he really wanted was not from the street level, but from above the building. To get this angle, Abe got permission to go on the roof of a downtown building that overlooked the Capitol. He took several photos and returned to the studio to begin sketching. A few days later, some agents, assumed to be from the Tennessee Bureau of Investigation, dropped by to ask Abe why he was taking photos of a government building. Abe immediately became a celebrity among his peers for his brush with Homeland Security.

3 The sketching stage was laborious. The antique style of poster design Abe was emulating required the line art and typography to be rendered entirely by hand. So he did an old-fashioned perspective drawing, complete with vanishing points that were taped to scraps of paper several inches outside of the actual composition. He hand-lettered the type and drew every detail of the building, creating cross hatching for shadows and shading.

4 The final step was to digitize the line drawings. Abe scanned the type, border art and the ink drawing of the building and pieced them together on his computer, an Apple G4. He added color in Photoshop, turning the black pen and ink line art into blue and red line art to play off of the Tennessee state flag colors. He also scanned some old paper so he could overlay the yellowed edges and aged textures onto his art, giving the entire poster a vintage look.

GENERAL JACKSON® SHOWBOAT

ON JUNE 23, 1985, thousands lined the riverbanks of the Cumberland to see a boat that's almost the length of a football field. Onlookers waved at the craft they'd heard so much about, the one painted red, white and blue with a theater that could hold 600 people.

The *General Jackson Showboat* was a sight to see that day, and for the past 22 years, the cruises have been a favorite of tourists and natives alike.

In 1983, Opryland USA, Inc. earmarked more than $12 million to build an elaborate showboat to use as another attraction. The Jeffersonville, Indiana company Jeffboat Inc., who also built the larger *Mississippi Queen*, was hired to construct the boat. About a year and a half later, a boat that measured 300 feet from gangplank to paddle wheel began its first sail down the Cumberland River. Named for the first steamboat to sail on the Cumberland River, the boat donned a 32-by-9 foot *General Jackson* logo on its exterior. The 1,489-ton boat's capacity can hold 1,200 passengers and 157 crew.

On the interior, 19th-century appeal was boosted by modern enhancements; the appearance and vibe of a

The General Jackson Showboat offers day and night cruises on the Cumberland River.

New Orleans Lounge, and the boat's showpiece, the Victorian Theatre, were reminiscent of the days of Mark Twain, but were now air conditioned.

In it's early years, riders on the *General Jackson* could pay $10 to $30, depending on the time of day, and travel between the four decks enjoying food, dancing, sightseeing and country or Broadway-style music performances. As popularity grew, the showboat became a favorite for private parties, and even weddings. Today, visitors can enjoy many different types of shows and events, including the popular holiday shows. However, tickets cost just a little bit more than they did in the late 80s.

While this majestic paddle wheel boat looks like an antique from the 1800s, it is a modern engineering marvel offering passengers lazy afternoon cruises under the southern sky, as well as evening cruises complete with entertainment, dining, and dancing under the stars. Featuring a spacious Victorian theatre, indoor and outdoor bars, observation decks that offer spectacular views of the Nashville skyline, banquet dining and dance floors, the *General Jackson* has become Music City's favorite floating landmark.

There was a time when steamboats like these came and went from Nashville every day.

< GENERAL JACKSON SHOWBOAT 18" x 24" Limited Edition Print created in 2005 by Abe Goolsby

"I did not have the luxury of time to hand draw this design like I had done on the Union Station or the State Capitol prints. So I started with a photo of the General Jackson and attempted to simulate a digital pen and ink effect on the computer. I still had to do a lot of illustration, but this time it was all done with a computer mouse instead of a pen. Come to think of it, I'm not sure that it really saved me any time when all was said and done — but it was fun to experiment with a different medium!"

VANDERBILT UNIVERSITY

ON THE SURFACE it would appear that noted journalist David Brinkley, champion basketball player Will Perdue, late actress Bettie Page, and former U.S. Vice President Al Gore would have nothing in common.

Original Main Building before it was destroyed in a fire.

But at one time or another, all four of these people were students at Vanderbilt University. Although they all went on to pursue very different careers, it gives an idea of the mass of diverse talent, and the level of success that's reached by the graduates of the university on 21st Avenue South.

Ironically, it was a successful man with little education that made Vanderbilt possible. Cornelius Vanderbilt gave one million dollars to start one of the finest Southern universities.

Vanderbilt traditionally did not entertain requests for money, but his wife helped her cousin, Methodist Bishop Holland N. McTyeire of Nashville, convince him to donate to the cause in 1873.

McTyeire chose the site for the new school, and supervised the construction. One building was erected to serve as an observatory and homes for professors. Landon C. Garland, the school's first chancellor, helped McTyeire set curriculum and policies. In 1873, the school's charter was amended, naming the school "The Vanderbilt University."

The main building burned in 1905, but was rebuilt and later named after the school's longest-serving chancellor, James Kirkland.

From day one, the school offered both undergraduate and graduate degrees in both the liberal arts and the sciences. For 40 years, the school was under the supervision of the Methodist Episcopal Church, but administrative differences would cause the two entities to split in 1914.

The school enrolled 307 students in the fall of 1875, and at least one woman would attend the school each year forward. Beginning in 1892, women worked for full legal equality and achieved it—except access to dormitories. By 1913, 78 women were Vanderbilt students; at this time they led the student body in grade point averages and university honors.

The school continued to grow, but still faced problems common to Southern universities at the time. In order to move the school forward, it fell to Chancellor Harvie Branscomb to push the school toward racial integration. The division of the campus after the dismissal of divinity student James Lawson in 1960, and changes in society at the time, would push the school to fully integrate in 1962. Other societal changes would influence university policy; in 1969, the quota that kept women to one-third of the enrollment in the College of Arts and Sciences was lifted.

Since the 60s, the campus has continued to grow and diversify. Today, Vanderbilt educates more than 10,000 students each year. It is also the largest private employer in Middle Tennessee, and still strives to reach Cornelius Vanderbilt's goal of contributing "to strengthening the ties which should exist between all sections of our common country."

Main Building was rebuilt and renamed Kirkland Hall.

< VANDERBILT UNIVERSITY   18" x 24" Limited Edition Print created in 2006 by Joel Anderson

"Historic Kirkland Hall stands proudly as the centerpiece of the oldest part of the Vanderbilt University campus. To render this print, I had to visit the site repeatedly to get just the right angle of sunlight. By the way, 7:45 am in the month of September is the best time to see Kirkland Hall as it appears in this poster!"

FISK UNIVERSITY

The Fisk Jubilee Singers circa 1872.

Fisk Jubilee Hall as it looked in the early 1900s.

MAJOR CONTRIBUTORS to the Harlem Renaissance. Trailblazers in politics. Key leadership in the Civil Rights Movement.

If you look back through pertinent periods in American history, there's a good chance that a Fisk University alumnus or professor had a hand in shaping it. When you read about modern art or jazz or science, it's likely that a Fisk graduate was the first one to do it, make it, sing it, write it or play it.

In it's 141-year history, the school has earned and retained a reputation for academic and artistic excellence, despite financial hardships; those well-trained graduates, such as James Weldon Johnson, John Lewis and Constance Baker Motley, have gone on to contribute not just to African-American history, but American history.

The creation of Fisk is a historical event in itself. Just six months after the end of the Civil War, John Ogden, education superintendent for the Freedmen's Bureau, Reverend Erastus Milo Cravath and Reverend Edward Smith established a school for former slaves. Union Army General Clinton B. Fisk provided Union Army barracks, near the present site of Union Station, to house the school, and the institution was named in his honor. The first classes at Fisk School were held January 9, 1866.

The next year, lawmakers passed legislation creating free public education in

Tennessee, and to meet the new demand for qualified teachers, Fisk moved its focus from primary education to higher education. On August 22, 1867, Fisk Free Colored School was incorporated as Fisk University.

The years that followed brought a surge in enrollment, but the funding couldn't keep up with the demand for infrastructure updates. In order to raise money to keep the school's doors open, George L. White, professor of music, created a nine-member choral ensemble of students and took it on tour. The group left campus on October 6, 1871, and used the contents of the school's treasury for travel expenses.

While on tour, the singers reached a point where they were physically and emotionally drained. To encourage them, White named them "The Jubilee Singers," a Biblical reference to the year of Jubilee in the Book of Leviticus. Incredible talent and dedicated work won over predominantly white audiences including Mark Twain, Ulysses S. Grant and Queen Victoria. Gradually they earned enough money to keep Fisk open and construct Jubilee Hall, which was designated as a National Historic Landmark in 1975.

Over the years, the addition of programs and resources has helped place Fisk as a renowned academic institution, producing such seminal figures in history as W.E.B. DuBois, Thurgood Marshall, John Hope Franklin and Nikki Giovanni. And after more than 100 years, the founders' dream of having a learning institution open to all, one that measures itself by "the highest standards, not of Negro education, but of American education at its best" is still a reality.

< FISK UNIVERSITY 18" x 24" Limited Edition Print created in 2007 by Joel Anderson

"The tower on the corner of the old Fisk building is one of my favorite steeples in Nashville. While shooting my reference photography, I felt as if I was on hallowed ground—I could sense the weighty historical and social importance of this great Nashville institution."

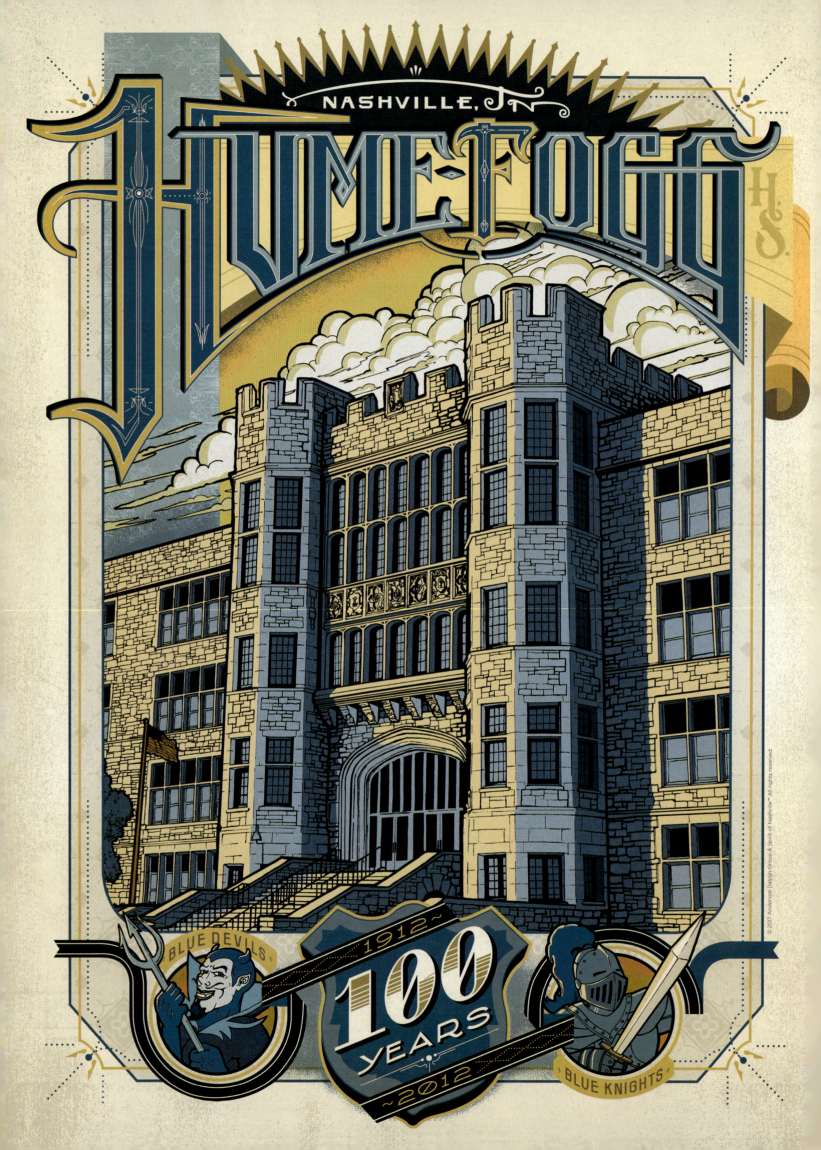

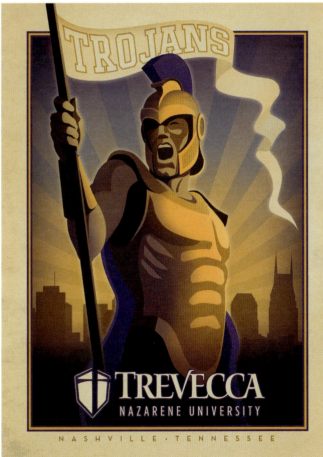
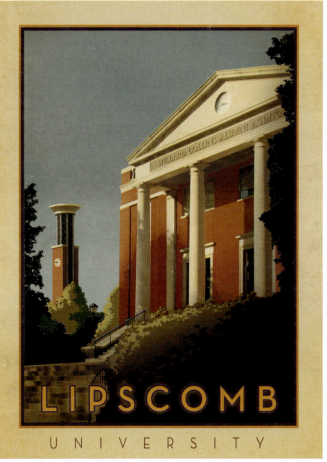

< HUME FOGG HIGH SCHOOL 18" x 24" Limited Edition Print created in 2011 by Andy Gregg
BELMONT UNIVERSITY 18" x 24" Limited Edition Print created in 2007 by Joel Anderson
WATKINS COLLEGE OF ART, DESIGN & FILM 18" x 24" Limited Edition Print created in 2010 by Joel Anderson
TREVECCA NAZARENE UNIVERSITY 18" x 24" Limited Edition Print created in 2008 by Joel Anderson
LIPSCOMB UNIVERSITY 18" x 24" Limited Edition Print created in 2007 by Joel Anderson

THE GREAT FLOOD OF 2010

This photo: Courtesy of Metro Nashville Archives

Photo below: Flood 2010 Digital History Collection, Nashville Public Library

IN A 36-HOUR PERIOD on May 1st and 2nd, 2010, Nashville broke almost every historical rainfall record as an epic storm system dumped over 13 inches of rain. Some areas reported receiving over 20 inches in just a day and a half. Of the 20 gauges that monitor river levels in Middle Tennessee, 13 showed the highest levels ever. Others failed when waters rose higher than the guages could register, and others were simply swept away. On May 2, 2010, the Cumberland River crested at 51.86 feet in downtown Nashville—almost 12 feet above flood stage.

The flood is estimated to have caused more than 2 billion dollars in damage to homes, businesses and city infrastructure. Almost 11,000 properties were damaged or destroyed—and more than half of them were outside the 100-year flood plain. 10,000 people were displaced from their homes, and 24 people died across Tennessee—11 of them were in Davidson County. 2,773 businesses were forced to close temporarily or permanently, affecting over 14,000 employees and costing 3.6 billion dollars in lost revenue. Thousands of dollars worth of vintage musical instruments and sound equipment were lost in storage

sites that were engulfed. It was the biggest disaster to ever hit the city of Nashville.

Almost immediately, volunteers mobilized all over the city to rescue stranded people, bring food and water to those who needed it, remove water-logged drywall, furniture, and debris, and comfort neighbors who had lost everything. The outpouring of generosity and care was simply astounding. Over 25,000 volunteers signed up for clean-up and repair efforts, freely giving over 332,000 hours of their time to help their fellow citizens. *The Community Foundation of Middle Tennessee* received over 14 million dollars in donations from individuals and organizations. Country singer Garth Brooks raised almost 5 million dollars through a series of benefit concerts.

The day after the flood, several of us helped remove debris from people's homes. After hundreds of volunteers poured into devastated neighborhoods to continue the reconstruction efforts, we returned to our design studio to put our skills to

---

PLAY ON FLOOD RELIEF POSTER   18" x 24" Limited Edition Print created in 2010 by Matt Lehman & Joel Anderson

"This was the second design we created to raise money for flood victims. Combined with the first print, we raised over $30,000."

> "I visited Anderson Design Group in search of your Play On poster commemorating the May 2, 2010 Flood. I was brought to tears by your kindness when you gave me the poster for free upon hearing my flood story. You even sent a print to my mother-in-law whose home was totally destroyed in Bellevue! It is kindness and generosity from people like you that got my family through the dark days after the flood. Nashville is the greatest city in America and the 'Spirit of Nashville' definitely shines brightly around here. Thank you with all my heart!" — **Cathy Wilson**

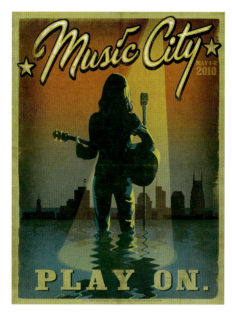

work creating art that we could sell to raise funds for flood victims. We initially created two posters with powerful symbolism—the first design featured two helping hands lifting a guitar out of the rising water. The second design was a quick re-tooling of an older Music City print featuring a female singer at a microphone. We illustrated water up to her knees and added the words PLAY ON to the bottom of the poster. That phrase became a rallying cry for all of Music City. It's what we do here in Nashville. The show must continue. Everyone we knew rolled up their sleeves and played on. No whining. No blaming. We just helped each other out, gave of our time, resources and energy, and did what needed to be done. Tennessee is the Volunteer State, after all!

A year later, we created a new print to commemorate the 1-year anniversary of the flood. This third design showed a mandolin drying out—only a drip and a small puddle remained. Flowers had bloomed from the broken strings. A bright golden sky symbolized the dawning of a new day. Nashville was different as a result of the adversity. While the flood was a terrible experience, it brought everyone together like nothing else could.

The tragic event activated our community and brought about a new sense of civic pride and volunteerism. *Hands On Nashville*, an organization that coordinated volunteers in the aftermath of the flood, and enlisted thousands of volunteers during the following months. To this day, they continue to connect over 120,000 volunteers each year with various community projects. We are truly stronger, better and brighter as a result.

The Harpeth River rose to record levels and swallowed up enitre neighborhoods. These photos were taken in Bellevue a few days after the flood.

HELPING HANDS FLOOD RELIEF POSTER 18" x 24" Limited Edition Print created in 2010 by Joel Anderson

"This was the first design we created to raise money for flood victims. We printed 500 of them and sold out in 3 weeks. Many people bought our commemorative prints to help friends or neighbors redecorate their homes after losing everything in the flood."

STRONGER. BETTER. BRIGHTER. (1-YEAR FLOOD ANNIVERSARY)   18" x 24" Limited Edition Print created in 2011 by Ligia Teodosiu

"Even one year after the flood, there were still people who were struggling to rebuild their homes and businesses. We wanted to continue to help them and to raise awareness that many of our fellow citizens still needed support to rebuild their homes or businesses."

MUSIC CITY USA

NASHVILLE
TENNESSEE

SINCE 1806

WHERE MUSIC
lives and breathes

MUSIC CITY USA

NASHVILLE HAS LONG been home to the country recording industry and the famous Grand Ole Opry. It's the place that popularized country music giants such as Johnny Cash, Patsy Cline, Hank Williams, Minnie Pearl, Roy Acuff, Dolly Parton and Loretta Lynn. Nashville was first called "Music City" by WSM announcer David Cobb during a radio broadcast in 1950, and is now known around the world as "Music City, U.S.A." City promoters have recently abbreviated Nashville's nickname as "Music City" in hopes of making the name even more catchy and easy to remember.

Over the years, Nashville's reputation as a mecca for music business, songwriting, recording, and performing has expanded to more than just country music. Today, Music City proudly boasts musical excellence in nearly every genre—from the grandeur of the Nashville Symphony to the mellow sounds of smooth club jazz; from the familiar twang of little honky-tonk country bands to stadium-filling Top 40 acts. Nashville is also home to several gospel music record label headquarters.

Nashville's music scene began to pick up momentum in the 1920s and 30s with the formation of the symphony orchestra and the Grand Ole Opry. The mid 1940s and early 1950s brought Country Music into full swing when the Opry moved to the Ryman, dubbing the old tabernacle "The Mother Church of Country Music."

Music Row began to take shape with the birth of new recording studios and record labels. Castle Studio, Nashville's first recording studio, opened for business. Capitol Records became the first major record label to station a director of country music in Nashville. Soon RCA Studio B opened it doors on Music Row and became famous under the management of Chet Atkins, who was instrumental in crafting the Nashville Sound.

Performers such as Elvis, the Everly Brothers and Dolly Parton recorded their chart-topping hits in Nashville. The Country Music Association was founded and The Country Music Hall of Fame and Museum was built on Music Row.

Over the years, Nashville's music scene has evolved into a diverse and vibrant industry, attracting new indie rock groups, alternative bands, and music production ventures for television and movies.

Today, aspiring songwriters and performers continue to flock to Music City to make a name for themselves, proving that no place sounds as good as Nashville, Tennessee.

Loretta Lynn, Johnny and June Carter Cash, and Chet Atkins are just a few of the many famous voices that helped turn Nashville into Music City.

Photos courtesy of the Nashville Public Library, The Nashville Room

> "*I love Nashville. I love that on any given day you might walk past the guy who wrote "Midnight Train To Georgia," "He Stopped Lovin' Her Today" or "Because He Lives." I love that the wide-eyed girl refilling your coffee cup, who just flew into town on a dream and a prayer, might be "the next big thing" but no one knows it yet. Nashville's been good to people who love music, it's been good to songwriters like me. It's the one town where the song still matters the most. That's what makes me get up every morning and try again. That's why I call it home.*"
> — **Connie Harrington, songwriter**

< MUSIC CITY (RED GUITAR)   18" x 24" Limited Edition Print created in 2007 by Taaron Parsons

"This print was based on a design I did as a student. I finished it at the last minute, and it was added to the 2007 Spirit of Nashville calendar and poster collection almost as an afterthought. It has turned out to be one of the more popular prints in the series."

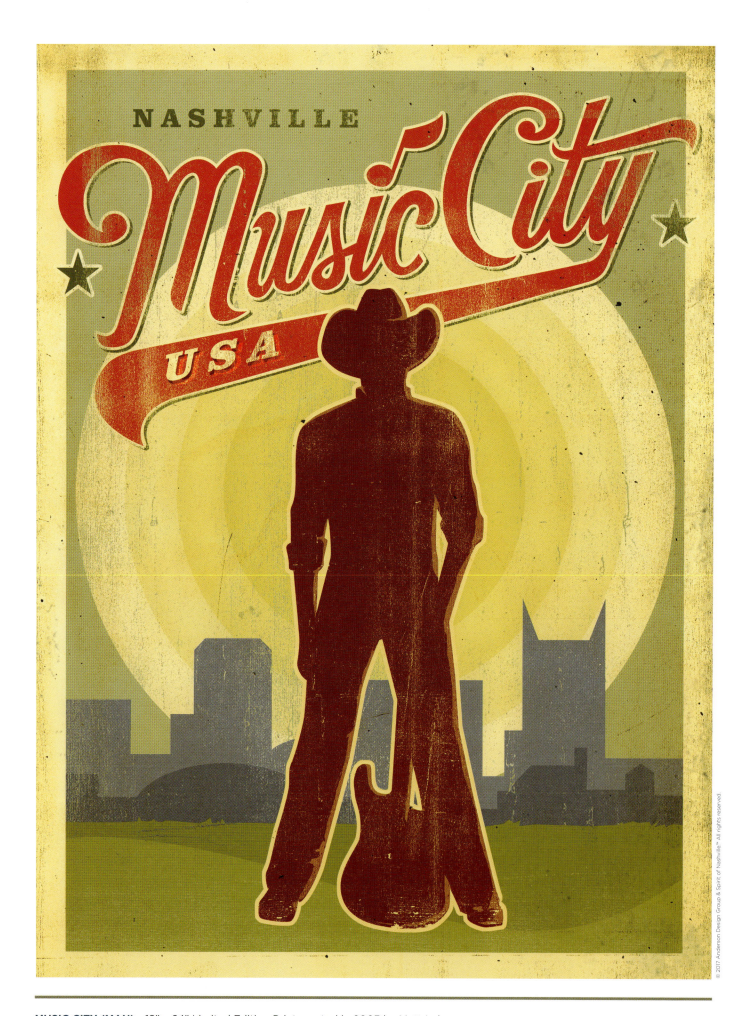

MUSIC CITY (MAN) 18" x 24" Limited Edition Print created in 2003 by Matt Lehman

"This was the first Music City theme in the collection. Due to its popularity with locals and tourists, we have done a new one each year."

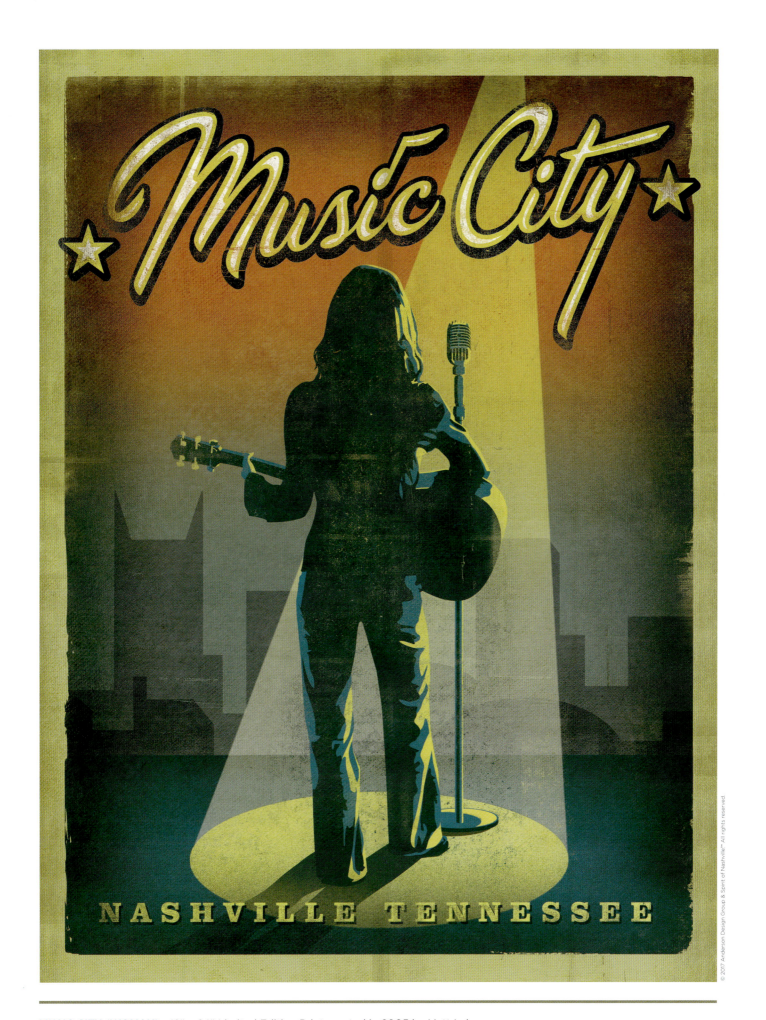

MUSIC CITY (WOMAN)   18" x 24" Limited Edition Print created in 2005 by Matt Lehman

"No, she is not someone famous... I needed a model in a hurry for this design, so I called my wife, Amber, and had her come to the studio and pose."

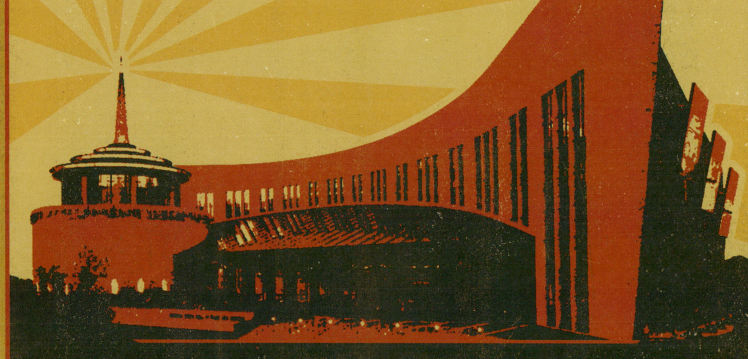

COUNTRY MUSIC HALL OF FAME® AND MUSEUM

IN 2007, the Country Music Hall of Fame® and Museum celebrated its fortieth anniversary as a not-for-profit educational institution, while also marking the sixth anniversary of its landmark new building at Fifth Avenue South and Demonbreun Street, the heart of downtown Nashville's sports and entertainment district.

Curving behind the glass of the building's Curb Conservatory and the indigenous stone of the facade are two block-long floors of gallery spaces where visitors discover the Museum's core exhibition, *Sing Me Back Home: A Journey Through Country Music*. This epic story traces country music history from its nineteenth century origins to its present-day cultural value. The Museum's vigorous changing exhibition schedule includes a major 5,000-square-foot installation that rotates every two years and a biographical cameo exhibit that generally honors a member of the Country Music Hall of Fame and opens each year in late summer. Throughout the Museum, visitors will find smaller exhibits of shorter duration spotlighting special country music anniversaries or new items in the collection. All changing exhibits amplify and expand the *Sing Me Back Home* story.

The building's rotunda, topped by a replica of the iconic 650 WSM diamond-shaped radio tower, houses the Museum's intimate Ford Theater on the ground floor. Above the theater, wreathed in clerestory windows and pierced by the bottom half of the radio tower, is the Country Music Hall of Fame exhibit, a circle of bronze plaques commemorating the lives and careers of those who have received country music's highest honor.

From major exhibitions to school programs, and from books and records to special events in the Ford Theater, research and scholarship inform the many offerings that have made the Museum a playground and learning lab for millions of visitors.

Over four decades, the Museum has amassed a country music collection generally considered the finest and most complete in the world. Accredited by the American Association of Museums since 1987, the institution's collection and the experts who care for it, interpret it, and make it publicly accessible are an eternal flame that validates and memorializes the lives of untold numbers of known and unknown musicians forever connected through the power of country music. So that we may be instructed and inspired by them, the Country Music Hall of Fame and Museum saves our songs of home, our common wealth, for the betterment of all mankind.

In 2014, a new 210,000 square-foot expansion was opened to showcase more of the museum's 2 million artifacts.

< COUNTRY MUSIC HALL OF FAME® AND MUSEUM   18" x 24" Limited Edition Print created in 2006 by Joel Anderson

"As simple as this poster looks, it was actually quite difficult to create. There are so many famous instruments, costumes, photos and artifacts in the Country Music Hall of Fame and Museum, but because of complicated permissions and copyrights, and the fact that hundreds of people are represented in the museum, we could not depict a famous person's face or single out any one performer's instrument to feature on the poster. So we settled on showing off the striking building along with the logo and now famous tag line, Honor Thy Music.™"

NASHVEGAS 18" x 24" Limited Edition Print created in 2006 by Darren Welch
MUSIC CITY PATTERN PRINT 18" x 24" Limited Edition Print created in 2010 by Joel Anderson
CMA MUSIC FESTIVAL 18" x 24" Limited Edition Print created in 2010 by Andy Gregg
MUSIC CITY (RECORDS) 18" x 24" Limited Edition Print created in 2007 by Darren Welch

LOWER BROADWAY, MUSIC CITY 18" x 24" Limited Edition Print created in 2012 by Andy Gregg & Joel Anderson

"This design was actually created as part of the Art & Soul of America series which celebrates great American Cities and travel destinations. Everyone liked the design so much that we decided to include it in the Spirit of Nashville Collection, too!"

BLUEBIRD CAFE

This is the original songwriter night audition form filled out for Garth Brooks. He autographed it for Amy Kurland, owner of the Bluebird.

YOU WOULD NEVER GUESS that this ordinary awning-covered storefront entrance is actually a doorway to fame. When you turn off of Hillsboro Pike into the Bluebird Cafe parking lot, it looks like nothing more than a neighborhood bar—with a line of people waiting to get in. When you go in, it's a small, eclectic place, with a stage, tables and chairs, and walls papered with autographed headshots of performers.

But unless you'd heard of the place before, you wouldn't know that the little place is nicknamed the "Ellis Island of Nashville" — it's the stage that every musical newcomer to Music City must cross.

Upon its opening in June of 1982, it was just a casual restaurant that featured live music at night. Three years later, Sunday Songwriters Night was added to help showcase new talent. By 1987, the focus had moved from food to music, hosting live music every night of the week.

"I decided to focus on singer-songwriters," said owner Amy Kurland. "I was interested in helping up-and-coming artists and songwriters get noticed."

Several famous stars such as Kathy Mattea, Faith Hill and Trisha Yearwood once performed on the Bluebird stage.

Garth Brooks also played at the Bluebird before he was discovered.

"When Garth Brooks first moved to town, he'd become friends with Tony Arata, who's a songwriter," Kurland said. "And one time Tony played a song in the early show, and Garth was really struck by it. Garth said that when he got a record deal, he was going to record that song. That song was "The Dance", and it became one of his most well-known songs."

Because of its reputation, "listening room" would be a better description of

---

< BLUEBIRD CAFE 18" x 24" Limited Edition Print created in 2006 by Darren Welch

"The Bluebird print was one of my favorite posters to work on. We tried several options including a guy sitting on a stool playing the guitar. It was a cool look but it didn't seem to represent all the different artists—both men and women—that perform at the Bluebird. So I came up with an original bluebird character that would represent all artists and give the design a fun and unique look. The fork and knife that we added to the composition communicates that the Bluebird is also a place to eat while you listen to music."

BLUEBIRD CAFE

> "Throughout all the years, this industry has changed a million times, and in a world of changing waters, we all look for a rock to stand upon. In my opinion, the songwriter is the foundation of music and the Bluebird is the rock on which that foundation sits. The Bluebird has my gratitude, and Amy Kurland has my respect and my love." — **Garth Brooks**

> "The Bluebird's the nest that's hatched many a gifted songwriter. If I sound like a fan, it's because I am. I've stood in line. I've played the stage, In the Round, sat in the crowd, and been the last one to leave. It will always hold a very special place in my memory." — **Keith Urban**

> "For performers, New York City has Carnegie Hall. Los Angeles has the Hollywood Bowl. London has the Royal Albert Hall. Nashville has the Ryman Auditorium. For the past twenty years, thank God, songwriters have had the Bluebird Cafe...It is truly the Mecca for all songwriters. Thanks, Amy, for giving all these songs a home." — **Vince Gill**

the Bluebird than a "bar" or "restaurant". Performers don't play cover songs, and there is no house band. More often than not, if you come to the Bluebird, you're hearing musical talent in its most pure form—a piano or guitar, and a voice. Because of that, the place's slogan is "Shhh!", because quiet is requested at all times during a performance.

Kurland said that while the Bluebird is a place of encouragement for the up-and-coming, the audience provides a mix of "love and honest feedback". While some have received standing ovations and never made it big, others got polite applause at the Bluebird and went on to write hit songs. What matters, Kurland said, is that an artist is driven to keep going, no matter the level of response.

And there are plenty of driven people at the Bluebird every week. Twenty-five years later, there are two shows a night, seven nights a week; 75 songwriters a week cross that stage.

"You know how the Ryman is the Mother Church of Country Music?" Kurland said. "Well, we're the 'little chapel in the woods.' We like to think we're the open door, and you'll get your chance here."

In 2008, Amy sold the Bluebird to the Nashville Songwriters Association International. On October 10, 2012, the club became an important fixture on the ABC TV hit drama *Nashville*.

A partial list of people who have performed on the Bluebird stage:

Mose Allison
Susan Ashton
Margaret Becker
Dierks Bentley
Karla Bonoff
Paul Brady
Lenny Breau
Garth Brooks
Brooks & Dunn
Mary Chapin Carpenter
Carlene Carter
Gary Chapman
Kenny Chesney
Guy Clark
Rita Coolidge
David Crosby
Steve Earle
Melissa Etheridge
Crystal Gayle
Patty Griffin
Emmylou Harris
Faith Hill
Indigo Girls
Alan Jackson
Carole King
Michael McDonald
Juice Newton
Maura O'Connell
Brad Paisley
John Prine
Kim Richey
Ray Stevens
Donna Summer
Bonnie Raitt
Rascal Flatts
Trisha Yearwood

This home-made poster appeared on a hundred telephone poles around town, announcing the Bluebird's grand opening. The Jay Patten Band, was the club's opening night act in 1982

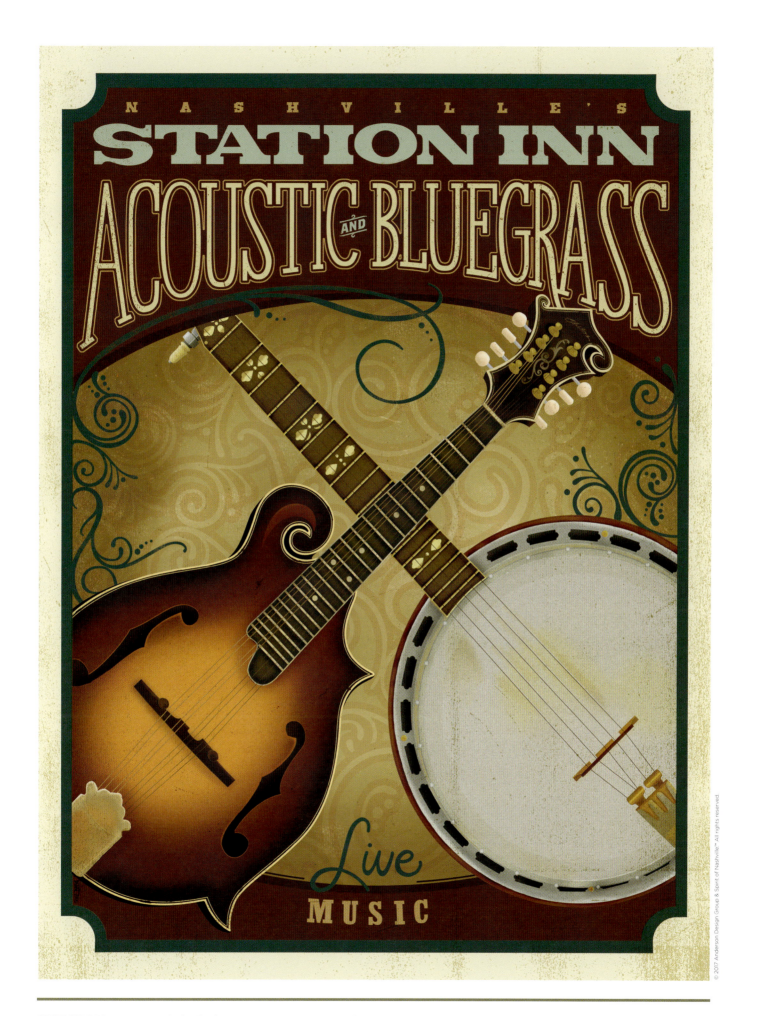

STATION INN 18" x 24" Limited Edition Print created in 2006 by Kristi Carter Smith

"As legendary as it is, the Station Inn's exterior is not much to look at, so I took inspiration from the signage for the lettering, and chose to keep the focus on the banjo and mandolin. The detail in the instruments had to be right because any mistake would be immediately obvious to a musician."

CHAMBERS GUITARS   18" x 24" Limited Edition Print created in 2005 by Darren Welch

"This iconic poster has become one of the flagship designs in the Spirit of Nashville Collection. Originally created to celebrate Chambers Guitars, a shop just a few blocks from our design studio, this image has become a favorite icon for Music City souvenirs such as t-shirts and coffee mugs."

MUSIC IN BLOOM 18" x 24" Limited Edition Print created in 2011 by Ligia Teodosiu

"There is a lovely rose garden across from the Music City Center and the Country Music Hall of Fame. Upon closer inspection, you'll notice that all of the flowers are specially cultivated varieties named after famous Country Music singers like Dolly Parton, Barbara Mandrell, Pam Tillis and more."

NASHVILLE SYMPHONY

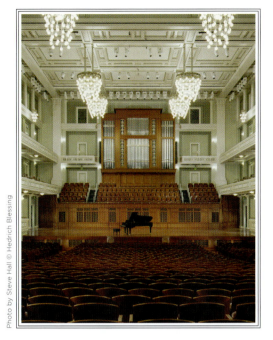

A STUNNING architectural icon spans an entire block in the heart of Nashville's entertainment district. The Schermerhorn Symphony Center, a beautiful, elaborate building that houses the Nashville Symphony, is a world-class performance hall, the envy of symphonies across the USA. Inside, ornate hallways lead you to a concert hall with an intimate atmosphere and a quality of sound like no other.

While the Symphony now flourishes, it definitely had a rocky start. The Symphony actually started in the 1920s when a group of amateur and professional musicians formed the Symphony Society, but the group would succumb to the hardships of the Great Depression.

But a young Nashvillian and music enthusiast would revive the idea of a symphony, literally campaigning for the money to restart it. Walter Sharp and his wife, Cheekwood heir Huldah Cheek Sharp, dreamed of creating a symphony in Nashville. While serving in the Army, Sharp met William Strickland, a fellow officer who'd done wonders with the Army band, and was convinced he was the man to lead Nashville's new orchestra. Strickland visited in 1946, upon his discharge from the service, and reactions from city leaders were encouraging. Sharp knew the true obstacle would be finances. But by the end of the summer of 1946, Sharp had more than 300 donors and $35,000 in start-up capital. Strickland was appointed as conductor in September 1946.

Strickland held auditions, and people from all walks of life tried out to be a member of the new symphony. When tickets went on sale for the first performance, people waited in line for two hours to buy them. The night of the performance, concertgoers were floored by the quality of the pieces; Strickland received four curtain calls.

Strickland left after the 1950-51 season; Guy Taylor (1951-1959), Willis Page (1959-1967), Thor Johnson (1967-1975) and Michael Charry (1976-1982) would succeed him. The Symphony moved from the War Memorial Auditorium to the Tennessee Performing Arts Center during Charry's tenure. In 1982, the Symphony created its following season with a series of guest conductors that would use their concerts as auditions for the top job. Kenneth Schermerhorn was a favorite and accepted the job in 1983. For 22 years, he led the Symphony through hardship and resurgence. Construction on the Schermerhorn Symphony Center began in 2003, but the respected conductor passed away in 2005, never seeing the full grandeur when it opened in September 2006.

Today, the Nashville Symphony gives more than 200 performances annually and is one of America's most productive recording orchestras. By 2014, the Nashville Symphony had already released 19 recordings, received a total of 14 GRAMMY nominations and won 7 GRAMMY awards.

< NASHVILLE SYMPHONY 18" x 24" Limited Edition Print created in 2006 by Taaron Parsons

"This poster was created just before the completion of the new Schermerhorn Symphony Center. The Symphony wanted us to feature the grand interior of the concert hall, but we needed to create the art before the grand opening. So I went to the hall during a closed performance to take reference photos. My wife posed in the studio as the violinist, and I had to create the crowd without the benefit of reference photos of a full house. I created the original illustration as an oil painting that we scanned so we could add typography and make some minor edits on the computer."

HOW THE ART WAS CREATED

Nashville Symphony   18" x 24" oil painting by Taaron Parsons

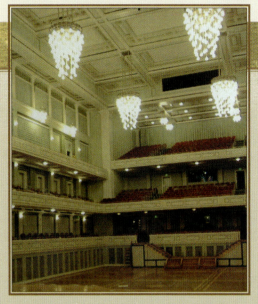

1 The first step in creating a poster design is to do some research and collect reference. As Anderson Design Group met with officials from the symphony, it became clear that the symphony needed to showcase the interior of the new performance hall, rather than the exterior of the building. Artist Taaron Parsons went to the empty hall before it was officially open to the public and took some reference photos. He was also invited to stand backstage during a special performance to observe the musicians from the angle he wished to paint. His concept was to create a view of the entire hall from behind the performers. Taaron's wife, Niki, posed for the violin soloist reference photo.

2 The next step was to sketch up possible poster concepts. Taaron began drawing a full orchestra, using his photographs for reference. After a few variations, he narrowed down the composition to just a few musicians surrounding a violin soloist. He planned to render his poster as an oil painting, so the composition needed to be figured out first in sketch form, and then redrawn onto a blank canvas before he could begin painting.

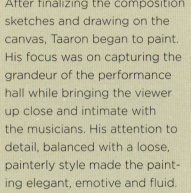

3 After finalizing the composition sketches and drawing on the canvas, Taaron began to paint. His focus was on capturing the grandeur of the performance hall while bringing the viewer up close and intimate with the musicians. His attention to detail, balanced with a loose, painterly style made the painting elegant, emotive and fluid.

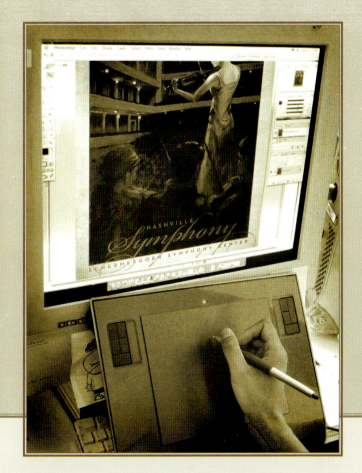

4 The final step was to digitize the oil painting, so it could be retouched and combined with typography on the computer. Because of the quick deadline for this poster design, Taaron had to carefully transport the wet oil painting to a photo studio where it was placed on a copy stand and photographed with a high-resolution digital camera. The photo of the painting was burned onto a CD, brought back to the Anderson Design Group studio, and loaded onto Taaron's work station, which at that time was an Apple G4 computer. He began retouching and color correcting the painting in Adobe Photoshop, darkening the background to draw more attention to the soloist. He then added typography, and a border. The final print-ready poster art was burned onto a CD and sent to McQuiddy Printing, where a limited edition run of 500 prints was produced.

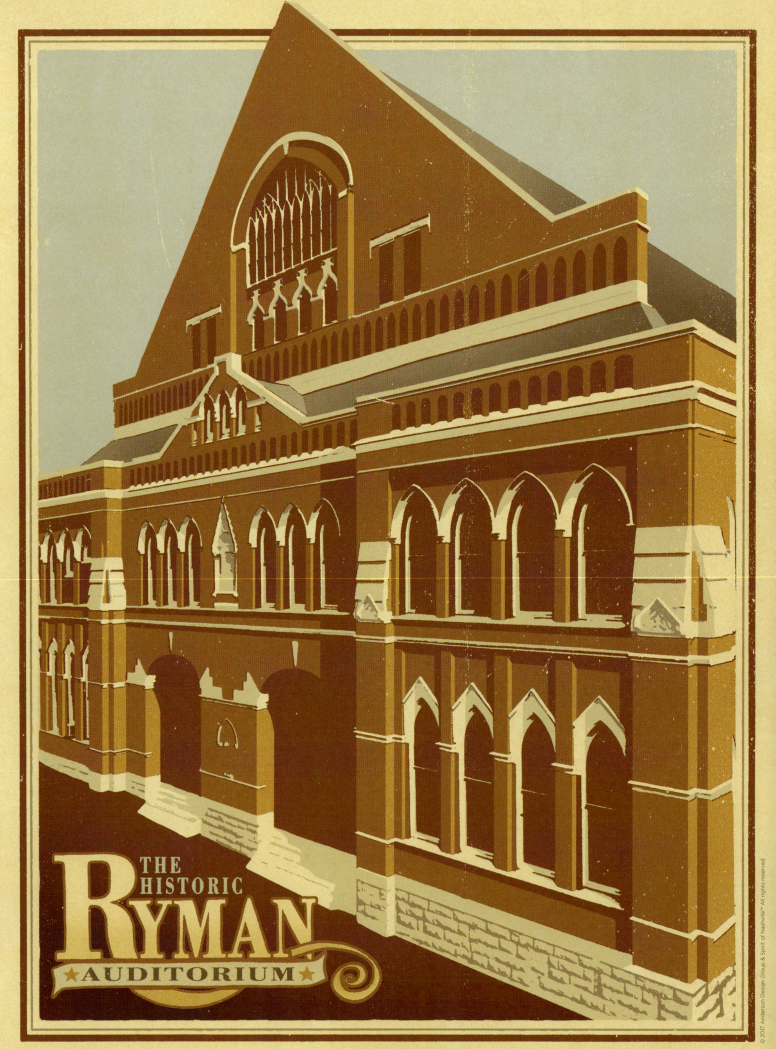

RYMAN AUDITORIUM

HAD REV. SAMUEL JONES never preached the gospel to a riverboat captain, there may never have been a Ryman Auditorium.

The popular evangelist converted Thomas G. Ryman to Christianity, and the former captain decided to build a venue to host the city's revivals. Ryman donated funds and Jones solicited additional monies to build the $100,000 Union Gospel Tabernacle. Nashville architect Hugh C. Thompson designed the Victorian Gothic building, and the first revival was held in May 1890, but the building wasn't completed until 1892. The pews, which are still used in the building, seated 3,755 attendees.

In order to have their conference there, the Confederate Veterans Association donated funds in 1897 to build an additional balcony. Known as the Confederate Gallery, the venue could now seat 6,000.

Ryman died in 1904, and Jones proposed the building should be renamed the Ryman Auditorium; the change was made official in 1944. For the next 40 years, the Ryman was the host of a number of concerts, plays, lectures, etc. President Theodore Roosevelt, John Philip Sousa, Isadora Duncan and countless others stood on the stage.

The Ryman gained national attention when the Grand Ole Opry began broadcasting from the venue in 1943. In 1963, National Life purchased the building and changed the name to the Grand Ole Opry House. Music greats such as Hank Williams, Sr., Elvis Presley, Johnny Cash, and Loretta Lynn all performed on the famous stage, until 1974, when the Opry moved to its current home at Opryland.

After the Opry left the Ryman, the venue went unused, except for the occasional concert. Although it was named to the National Register of Historic Places in 1971, the building almost faced demolition. It was saved, but greatly deteriorated from little use.

In the early 90s, Gaylord Entertainment commissioned architectural firm Hart Freeland Roberts to restore the Ryman. In June of 1994, after an $8.5 million renovation, the Ryman opened once again as a performance hall. Since then, the venue has hosted an increasingly diverse lineup, with musicians and performers from all genres taking the stage.

But no matter who's on stage, the Ryman will always be known as "The Mother Church of Country Music." Country legend Merle Haggard said: "You know, when you're standing there, you're on the sacred ground where all the grand old masters of country music have played."

Show prints promoting events at the Ryman.

< RYMAN AUDITORIUM 18" x 24" Limited Edition Print created in 2006 by Wayne Brezinka and Joel Anderson

"We started on this poster design using an old photo of the Ryman that was shot in the 1950s. At that time, there were some ugly additions to the building's grand doorways, which we had to paint out when we created the poster illustration. We chose a simplified color palette to make the poster more old fashioned and iconic, reminiscent of the days when the Grand Ole Opry called this magnificent old building home."

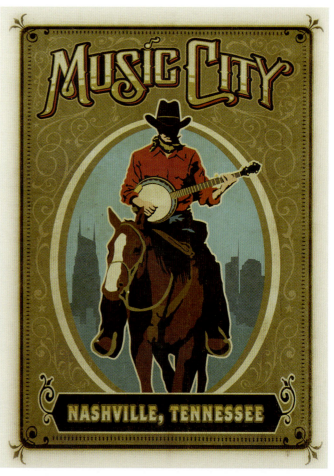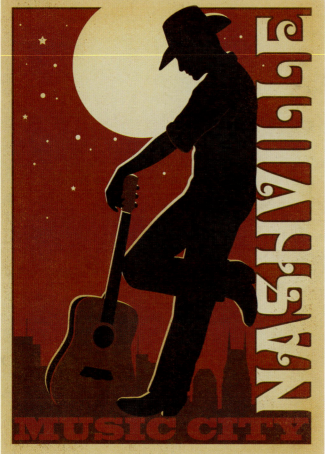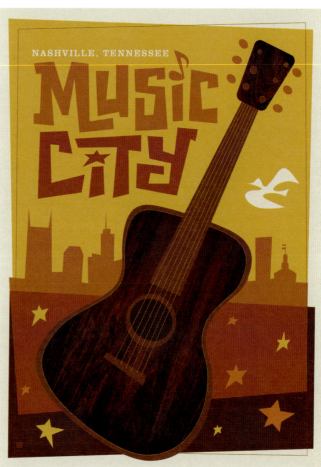

MUSIC CITY (GUITAR & MANDOLIN) 18" x 24" Limited Edition Print created in 2009 by Joel Anderson
MUSIC CITY (HORSE) 18" x 24" Limited Edition Print created in 2006 by Matt Lehman
MUSIC CITY DREAMING (LEANING COWBOY) 18" x 24" Limited Edition Print created in 2009 by Joel Anderson
MUSIC CITY (MOD) 18" x 24" Limited Edition Print created in 2014 by Joel Anderson

MUSIC CITY (PINUP GIRL)   18" x 24" Limited Edition Print created in 2008 by Joel Anderson

"This print pays homage to the sweetly evocative aircraft art that kept American airmen fighting for our country and longing for home."

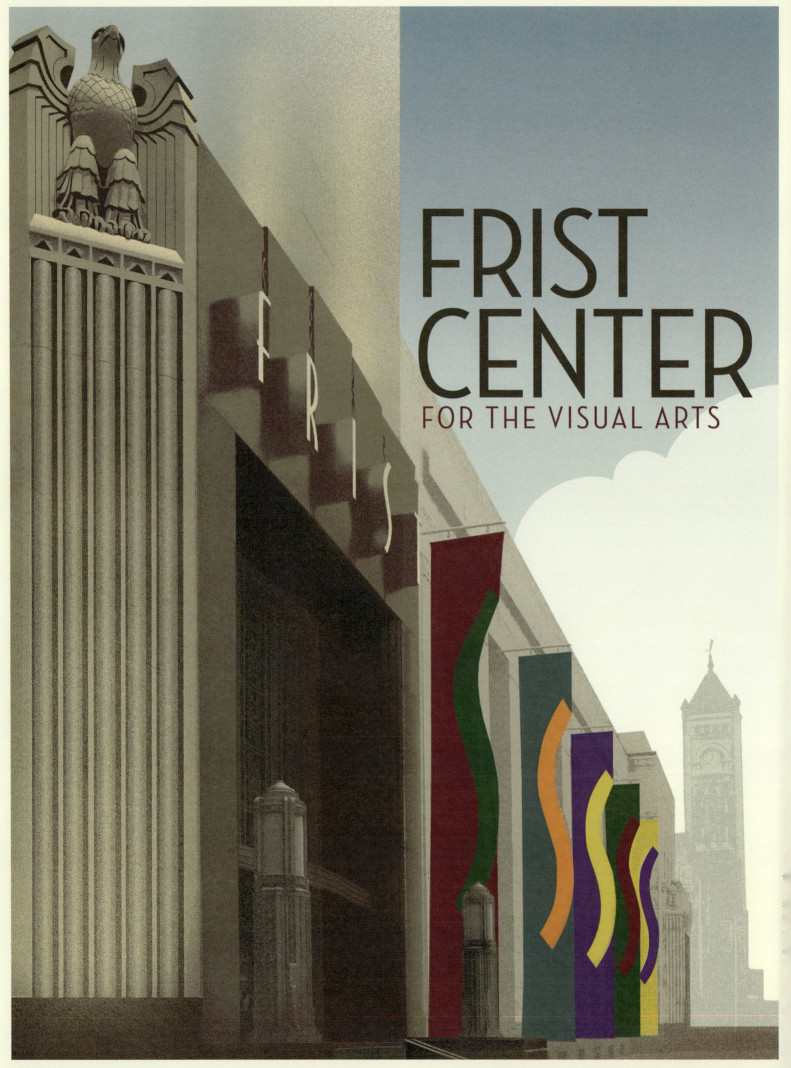

FRIST CENTER FOR THE VISUAL ARTS

The interior lobby area looks very much as it did when it was built as a post office.

IT WAS THE GENEROSITY of a well-known Tennessee family that made it all possible. Having taken their children to museums during their travels, Dr. and Mrs. Thomas F. Frist, Jr. recognized the importance of art and cultural education for children and families. So in the early 1990s, they decided to focus efforts toward the creation of an art center that would not only entertain, but also educate.

Residents and officials had thrown about the idea of an art facility for almost 25 years, but it was the results of a 1993 citizen effort entitled Nashville's Agenda that would move the idea for a center toward reality. In polling Nashvillians on how to make the city better, several cited the need for a downtown fine art facility. In 1994, Nashville's Agenda formed a steering committee to research the issue. Upon seeing the committee's report, Dr. Frist and Ken Roberts decided to take the lead in the attempt to create a major visual arts institution for the city, and the discussions began.

With education and community outreach as core emphases, it became clear that the location of the new institution should be located in the downtown area, on a major thoroughfare, and readily accessible. Since 1986, when the city's main post office relocated to an area near the airport, the U.S. Postal Service had only been utilizing a part of the first floor of their building on Broadway. The Frist Foundation contracted a Toronto-based firm to see if the building would suit their needs, and they reported that the building's structure would be ideal for a center. The Frist Foundation then entered into a partnership with the U.S. Postal Service, the city of Nashville, and the Metropolitan Development and Housing Agency to purchase the building that would become the Frist Center for the Visual Arts. MDHA leases the building to the Frist Center for one dollar a year for 99 years.

Financed through funds from the Hoover administration, the building was erected in 1933 and 1934 under the supervision of architectural firm Marr and Holman. The building's exterior, outfitted in white Georgia marble, exemplifies the classical style popular during the period, but the colored marble and aluminum grillwork in the interior represents the art deco style of the day. During renovations, it was paramount that the building's original character be maintained. Both the Frist family and the foundation pledged at least $25 million to bring the building to the highest museum standards.

Today, the 125,000 square-foot building not only exhibits visual art from local, state, regional, U.S. and international sources, but also offers a variety of programs and activities, including educational programs for children and adults, lectures, concerts and music.

Exterior of the former main post office, constructed in 1933-34.

< FRIST CENTER FOR THE VISUAL ARTS 18" x 24" Limited Edition Print created in 2004 by Joel Anderson

"This building is a work of art. Covered inside and out with stylized relief sculptures and beautiful metal work, there is no way to capture it all in a poster. Another challenge was trying to fit the horizontal building into our vertical poster format. We settled on a perspective of the Broadway face of the building which leads the eye to Union Station's tower. I rendered the poster in an Art Deco style to match the building."

CHEEKWOOD

BOTANICAL GARDEN
& MUSEUM OF ART

NASHVILLE, TENNESSEE

CHEEKWOOD BOTANICAL GARDEN & MUSEUM OF ART

The Wisteria Arbor.

A view of the Japanese garden; a mere fragment of the vast gardens and galleries at Cheekwood.

WITH LUSH GARDENS and a stately mansion spread across 55 acres, the Cheekwood Botanical Garden is just as breathtaking as when it was first built more than 70 years ago.

Each year, visitors make their way through this Nashville landmark, taking in the sea of tulips or a lovely stretch of wildflowers. Inside the mansion, people can marvel at pieces from the Permanent Collection, including a sculpture by Nashville sculptor William Edmondson.

And to think coffee started it all.

Leslie Cheek moved to Nashville in 1890 with his family to join his father's grocery business in Cummins Station. By 1892, the Cheeks were focusing on coffee; Leslie's cousin, Joel, had developed a blend of coffee, and members of the family invested to help support the new venture. In 1904, the Cheeks partnered with James Neal, and expanded the coffee line to other parts of the country. Joel was able to sell the best hotel in town, the Maxwell House, on their coffee, and they agreed to serve it exclusively. The coffee would now become known as Maxwell House coffee. Joel sold the coffee brand to Postum (now known as General Foods) in 1928, and profited $40 million. Leslie's investment in the once-fledgling business had now paid off.

Leslie would take the more than $1 million he gained from the sale, and build a home for his wife, Mabel Wood, whom he'd married in 1896. The Cheeks hired Bryant Fleming, a sought-after residential and landscape architect from New York, to build it. Fleming's philosophy was that the architecture, design, décor and landscaping should work together to make a unified statement. Fleming and the Cheeks traveled to Great Britain to find furnishings for the home; it took four railroad cars to bring back all they'd

A group of curious ladies awaits the opening of the Cheekwood Fine Art Center in 1960.

purchased. The 30,000 square-foot Georgian-style mansion was completed in 1932; the construction of Cheekwood was one of the largest employers during the Great Depression.

Leslie only lived in the home two years, and died in 1935. Mabel lived in the home another nine years, and then deeded the home to her daughter, Huldah, and her husband, Walter Sharp. In 1957, the Sharps offered the mansion and 55 acres of land to create a botanical garden and fine arts center. After renovations, Cheekwood opened May 22, 1960. The dedication was given by Senator Albert Gore, Sr.

Major renovations were made in the late 1990s to elevate the museum's standards. Special attention was paid to restore the original architecture and landscaping of the mansion. Today, Cheekwood continues to strive to fulfill its mission, to "inspire and educate by making art, horticulture, and nature accessible to a diverse community. Attracting over 300,000 visitors each year, Cheekwood is considered to be one of the top 10 public gardens in North America.

< CHEEKWOOD BOTANICAL GARDEN AND MUSEUM OF ART 18" x 24" Limited Edition Print created in 2003 by Joel Anderson

"Since Cheekwood's mansion, sprawling botanical gardens, art galleries, vistas, trails, green houses and sculpture gardens could make up an entire series of prints, we had to try to capture the essence of Cheekwood. This composition features a lady in the period attire of when the Cheek family called this beautiful estate home. The view is from the boxwood maze looking out over the hills of West Nashville."

NASHVILLE BALLET

Rachel Ellis as the Snow Queen in Nutcracker.

Sadie Harris in Ploughing The Dark *during* 2007 Bluebird Cafe at The Ballet 2.

EVERY CHRISTMAS SEASON, both novices and aficionados of ballet file into the Tennessee Performing Arts Center to see the annual holiday story they know well. But whether they've seen it once or a hundred times, ballet-goers are always amazed by the grace, technique and beauty of the Nashville Ballet's Nutcracker. As the Nashville Symphony sets their movements to music, viewers are drawn into the visual and aural experience that is the ballet.

Perhaps that's why Nashville Ballet is the second largest performance arts organization in Nashville.

And, it only took 25 years to get to that point. Started in 1981 as a small group of volunteers, the Nashville Ballet was originally called The Young Dancers Concert Group. They held their first spring concert in 1983 in the then-brand-new TPAC. Peggy Burks was hired as the artistic director, and in 1984, there was enough support to establish the group as an independent civic organization. The name was changed to Nashville City Ballet, and they offered two shows a year. The group became a professional company in 1986.

Artistic director Dane LaFontsee took the ballet's productions and performances to the next level; by the late 80s, the ballet was staging larger, more well-known story ballets such as Cinderella and Nutcracker.

And the audiences responded. The ballet's popularity continued to grow, and Paul Vasterling's promotion as artistic director in 1998 really catapulted the company, putting them on the national scene.

Providing world-class classical and contemporary ballet productions, Nashville Ballet pays homage to its Music City roots by working with local performers. Bluebird Cafe at the Ballet has become a popular performance where dancers bring the songs of local songwriters and musicians to life. Vasterling also pairs with up-and-coming talent, working with faculty at Vanderbilt's Blair School of Music on Emergence!, a presentation of original dance and music.

Today, the company employs 17 full-time dancers and five apprentices. Another 20 dancers are enrolled in the ballet's two-year, pre-professional program, and perform over 150 outreach and education programs for more than 30,000 children a year. The ballet's mission is to create, perform, promote and educate about dance.

"Nashville Ballet rounds out the cultural scene in Nashville," said Paul Vasterling, Artistic Director for the company. "Lots of people think of Nashville only as Music City. When people come to a performance, the majority of them are surprised and impressed with the high level of dance that Nashville Ballet delivers, illustrating that Nashville offers its wonderful music and so much more."

< NASHVILLE BALLET   18" x 24" Limited Edition Print created in 2005 by Kristi Carter Smith

"I chose to use a very loose and impressionistic illustration style for this poster in order to convey the energy of the ballerina. I rendered her in conté (a chalky artists' crayon), watercolor, and Photoshop."

NASHVILLE BASEBALL 18" x 24" Limited Edition Print created in 2003 by Darren Welch
Nashville's love for baseball goes all the way back to 1860 when Union soldiers first introduced the game to the local community. The most successful team to ever play here is the current team, the Nashville Sounds. Their new state-of-the-art ballpark is located in historic Sulphur Dell, which is the former site of Athletic Park, built in 1870. Baseball was played there for nearly 100 years, from 1870 to 1963.

McCABE GOLF COURSE 18" x 24" Limited Edition Print created in 2011 by Joel Anderson & Darren Welch

"McCabe is a public course that is built on what used to be an old airfield. Their logo includes an old airplane, so we added it to the sky in a nostalgic nod to the past. The golfer is wearing classic attire, even though the clubhouse in the distance is the current modern structure."

HATCH SHOW PRINT

IT'S AN UNDERSTATEMENT to say Hatch Show Print makes posters.

When you see one of their posters, it's like seeing a Nashville icon—you recognize the style, and you know exactly where it came from.

Since its founding in 1879, the printer has produced bold advertisements in bright colors for some of entertainment's most well-known acts. But early on, the posters surpassed their primary use as an information tool, becoming a symbol of both American and Southern culture.

In 1875, William Hatch moved his family from Wisconsin to Nashville. His two sons, Charles R. and Herbert H., had worked in their father's print shop, and intended to use their skills in letterpress printmaking to open a shop in Nashville. Four years after their arrival, the sons opened C.R. & H.H. Hatch; their first job was a handbill announcing a lecture by Rev. Henry Ward Beecher, brother of Harriet Beecher Stowe, for a dollar at the Grand Opera House.

The print shop's popularity grew, and it was not uncommon to see a sea of posters covering brick building walls and wooden light poles, announcing baseball games or concerts. Although some of their work was simple advertisements for grocery stores and movie theatres, they nonetheless served as a distinguishing brand for those businesses. Ironically, it was one of their own advertisements, placed in the December 1920 edition of the entertainment trade magazine *The Billboard*, which would first show the term "Hatch Show Print" in bold letters.

Floor to ceiling shelves hold thousands of vintage wood block letters and photo plates.

Manager Jim Sherraden pulls a classic Hatch poster reprint off the press.

The business really entered its heyday when Charles' son, Will, took over. Until his death in 1952, Will worked in the shop right behind the Ryman Auditorium and, by carving wood blocks, created some of the most recognizable images in entertainment, especially country music. Some of his biggest customers were Roy Acuff and Bill Monroe, who always wanted him to make a poster for their shows at the Grand Ole Opry. Will also did posters for some of the African-American stars of the era, such as Cab Calloway and Bessie Smith. Posters were printed for local events, such as Fisk Jubilee Singers' performances, and Vanderbilt University games, and big-name acts, like Elvis Presley and Hank Williams.

After Will's death, ownership of Hatch Show Print would change hands several times. In 1992, Gaylord Entertainment donated Hatch to the Country Music Hall of Fame® and Museum. Much effort was made to keep the print shop true to form as they made the move from their long-time home on Fourth Avenue North to the Mayfair Furniture building on Broadway.

Today, guided by the motto "Preservation Through Production," Hatch Show Print is a working print shop, owned and operated by the Country Music Hall of Fame and Museum. The crowded shop still houses more than 10,000 wood blocks, drawers filled with wood and metal type, and 14 presses. They still crank out more than 600 jobs a year for a myriad of acts and events, leaving no doubt that a little print shop in Nashville, Tennessee, is still in big demand.

< HATCH SHOW PRINT 18" x 24" Limited Edition Print created in 2007   by Emily Keafer

"It was a surprise and an honor to be asked by Hatch Show Print if we would create a poster that featured their historic establishment. I have been a fan of this legendary print shop since college, when I attended a presentation by Hatch manager Jim Sherraden. It was a challenge to determine the subject matter for the print. I didn't want to mimic their distinct style, since that wouldn't pay homage as much as rip them off. So I decided to focus on the process of the art letterpress, depicting instead a printer hard at work over his press."

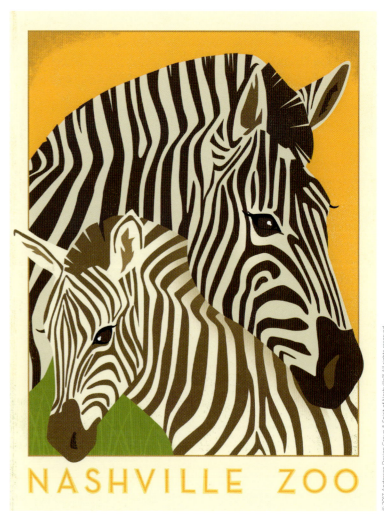

NASHVILLE ZOO

WILDLIFE IN NASHVILLE is abundant in the Nashville Zoo at Grassmere. It's a staple field trip spot for kids and adults alike, thanks to the friendly staff, outstanding playground, and wide variety of animals from around the world.

The Nashville Zoo opened in 1991 in Cheatham County and has experienced tremendous growth ever since. In 1996, Nashville Zoo took over management of the Grassmere property. Led by then-Mayor Phil Bredesen, the city offered Nashville Zoo the opportunity to relocate the Zoo from Joelton, TN and develop a "new" zoo for Nashville on the Grassmere property. In 1997, the Nashville Wildlife Park at Grassmere opened to the public under Nashville Zoo management. It featured a 66,000 sq. ft. Jungle Gym—the largest community-built playground in the United States. In 1999, Entry Village was added, featuring a gift shop and restaurant. In 2000, Critter Encounters, the Zoo's first interactive exhibit, opened. In 2004, the Zoo received accreditation from the Association of Zoos and Aquariums (AZA). In 2005, the 3.2 acre African Elephant Savannah opened and won exhibit of the year. Lorikeet Landing, the Zoo's second interactive exhibit, and the Wild Animal Carousel also opened that year. In 2006, the Giraffe Savannah exhibit and the Alligator Cove exhibit opened. In 2010, the Flamingo Lagoon exhibit opened, and in 2011, the Wilderness Express Train was added. 2013 saw the Kangaroo Kickabout open, and a 10 million dollar donation kicked off a capital campaign in 2014 that promised to take the zoo to new heights.

Today, the 6,230+ featured animals, which include red pandas, clouded leopards, African elephants, giraffes, zebras, flamingos, and komodo dragons, have helped make the Nashville Zoo the #1 attraction in Middle Tennessee. Students and families from all walks of life are drawn to the Zoo every year—attendance in 2013 alone exceeded 775,000 people!

With the help of 2,600 volunteers, the Nashville Zoo continues to grow as one of Music City's favorite places to visit.

Photo by David Bailey, courtesy of the Nashville Zoo

Photo by Jim Bartoo, courtesy of the Nashville Zoo

< NASHVILLE ZOO POSTER SERIES 18" x 24" Limited Edition Prints created in 2004-2007 by Kristi Carter Smith

"We created a new zoo print each year for 4 years in a row. People ask us how we decided which animals to feature in our art, since there are so many great species to choose from. In an effort to help the zoo promote new exhibits, we picked animals that were new to Nashville. We thought they probably wouldn't mind the extra attention since newcomers often need a little help when making new friends!"

Chaffin's BARN
DINNER THEATRE

Since 1967

THE "NASHVILLE WAY" TO ENJOY DINNER AND A PLAY!

CHAFFIN'S BARN DINNER THEATRE

Photos and artifacts courtesy of Janie Chaffin

Photos, an invitation, and a matchbook from the Barn's first years in business.

A DINNER THEATRE in a barn? That's an unusual entertainment venue! Some may think that dinner theatres—barns, or no barns—are obsolete, but the steady popularity of Chaffin's Barn Dinner Theatre would prove them wrong.

For the past 40 years, eager crowds have come to the big red barn off Highway 100 for both the all-you-can-eat Southern-style buffet and the Broadway-style shows. As soon as they walk in the door, the aromas of home-cooked food and chocolate chip cookies greet them. Crisp white tablecloths and small lamps surround the buffet area which, after the hearty dinner, is cleared to make room for the stage which descends from the ceiling. For the rest of the evening, the audience is mesmerized by the professional play taking place only a few feet away from them.

In 1967, not many in the Nashville area had experienced the dinner theatre concept, but a New York promoter convinced John and Edna Lou (Puny) Chaffin that such a venue would do well. They built the barn, and it was an instant success. At the outset, all plays were produced in New York, and a traveling theatre troupe performed at dinner theatre venues across the country.

John P. Chaffin purchased the Barn from his parents in 1976 and changed the name to Chaffin's Barn Dinner Theatre. All productions are now directed at Chaffin's using a mix of local and national actors. Chaffin's is individually owned and operated by John and his wife, Janie, who produce nine or ten shows each season. They are very proud to own and operate Nashville's first professional theatre. Over the years, the Barn has not only offered great dinner theatre, but it has also hosted fund-raisers, fashion shows, high school and college proms.

Shows are performed on the descending "magic stage" or in the more traditional Backstage theatre, which provides a more intimate atmosphere. Because of the close proximity of the actors and audiences, patrons say there's a family atmosphere to the place. The waiters (actors not in a current production) serve the audience, often acknowledging birthdays or anniversaries.

It's that family feel that keeps people coming back year after year. Chaffin's becomes a tradition, as the birthdays of children and grandchildren, anniversaries, graduations and other memorable milestones are celebrated at the big red barn. While Chaffin's is definitely in the theatre business, its first priority is to provide a fun environment where memories are made every time.

CHAFFIN'S BARN   18" x 24" Limited Edition Print created in 2007 by Darren Welch

"When people think of Chaffin's Barn Dinner Theatre, they mention the bright red barn, the intimate setting for enjoying live theatre or the giant buffet. We chose to render this print in a style similar to the Bluebird Cafe poster, symbolically representing the venue with the barn, the theatre with the masks and the food with the fork and plate that doubles as the moon."

BELLE MEADE THEATRE   18" x 24" Limited Edition Print created in 2004 by Joel Anderson
MUSIC CITY TROLLEY HOP   18" x 24" Limited Edition Print created in 2014 by David Anderson
NASHVILLE ROLLERGIRLS   18" x 24" Limited Edition Print created in 2014 by Aaron Johnson
THE LOVELESS BARN   18" x 24" Limited Edition Print created in 2010 by Andy Gregg & Joel Anderson

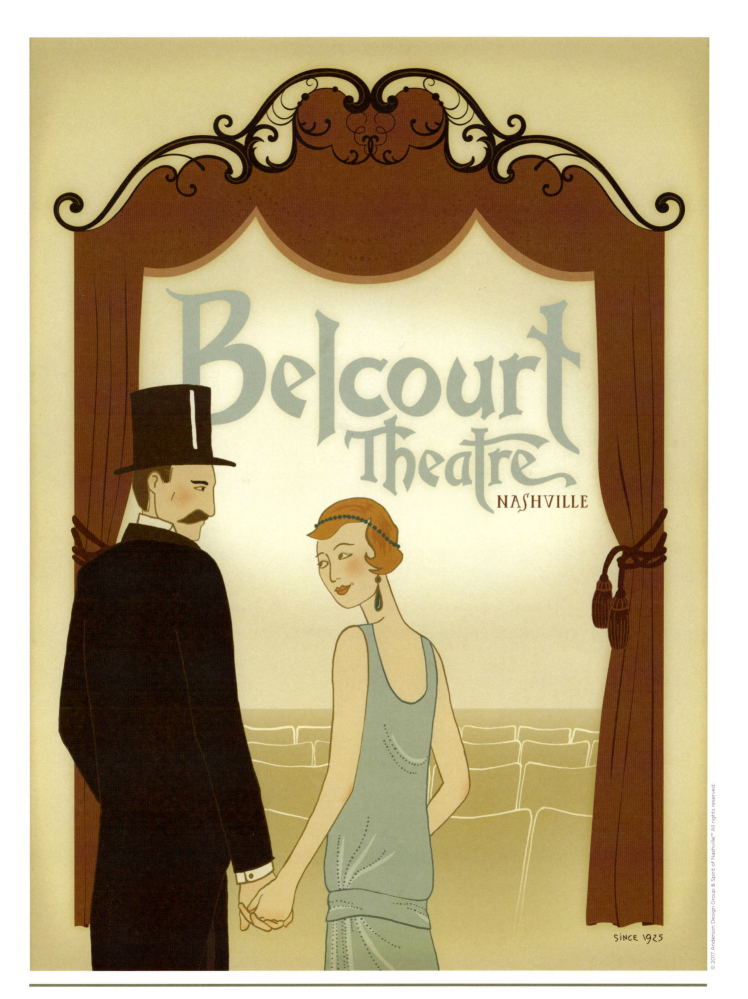

BELCOURT THEATRE 18" x 24" Limited Edition Print created in 2005 by Emily Keafer

"I've attended many films and events at the Belcourt since moving to Nashville, so I was thrilled to have the opportunity to create a poster for the historic theatre. I took inspiration from the work of George Barbier, a French illustrator whose work was contemporary to the opening of the theatre in 1925. The abstract stage and the couple in period dress gave the poster its unique charm and sets the look apart from the rest of the collection."

NASHVILLE SHAKESPEARE FESTIVAL

Scenes from Shakespeare in the Park *productions featuring fresh new settings and costumes for classic Shakespearian plays.*

ON THE WEEKENDS of August and September, Centennial Park becomes a sea of beach blankets and lawn chairs, as people settle in to enjoy Shakespeare against a sunset-filled sky.

For 20 seasons, people from all different walks of life have congregated at the well-known park off of West End Avenue to enjoy the various works of The Bard, staged by The Nashville Shakespeare Festival. During the 2006 season, more than 12,000 people saw one of the Festival's inventive interpretations of the famed poet's works.

Eclectic crowds spread out on blankets and lawn chairs to picnic and enjoy a play.

And while the Festival has enjoyed steady growth and success, the company's start was a grassroots effort. In 1988, a group of local actors who'd long dreamed of having a Shakespearean theatre company pooled their resources to start one. With $500 and no technical support, their first production of As You Like It drew 1,000 attendees over six performances. The founders were encouraged by the public's response, and since then, the company has focused on providing high-quality, full-scale productions of classics to people of all cultural and socioeconomic backgrounds at no cost. Some crowd favorites include *A Midsummer Night's Dream*, where the company set the play during the 1960s Summer of Love; the audiences loved the way Shakespeare's themes of conservatism vs. teen rebelliousness worked into that era. Another favorite is a Maxfield Parrish-inspired *Twelfth Night*. The romance of the 1920s was enhanced by an opera singer with a choir of little girls dressed in white with flowers in their hair.

The imagination and creativity of the company translated well in another venue: the classroom. Responding to the Metro Schools' need for an arts-in-education program, in 1992 the company developed 50-minute versions of some of Shakespeare's best-known works and took them into the schools. Now more than 130,000 students, many of whom had never seen live theatre, have had the experience, thanks to The Nashville Shakespeare Festival. That collaboration has led to partnerships with the Nashville Institute for the Arts and the Tennessee Performing Arts Center's Humanities Outreach in Tennessee, bringing theatre to even more fresh audiences.

But the Centennial Park performances are still the company's main draw, providing a perfect opportunity for a casual date or a family outing. People come back year after year because it's affordable, accessible, and reliable entertainment, and most importantly, they know they'll have a great time.

< NASHVILLE SHAKESPEARE FESTIVAL 18" x 24" Limited Edition Print created in 2007 by Kristi Carter Smith

"In this poster design, we were asked to reference the Festival's logo which features William Shakespeare with stars in his eyes. The Shakespeare in the Park events bring all kinds of people together in Centennial Park, so illustrating William lounging in shorts with his dog in front of the Parthenon seemed to say it all."

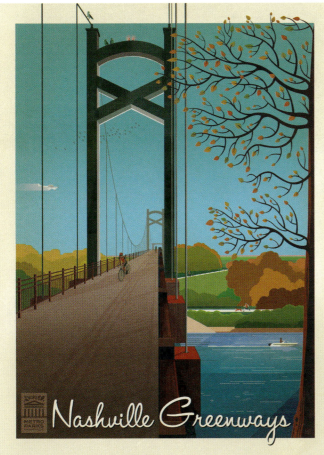
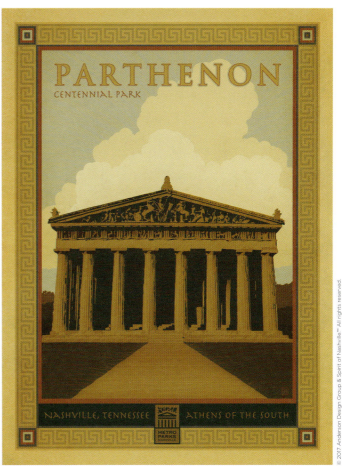

< FORT NEGLEY   18" x 24" Limited Edition Print created in 2011 by Andy Gregg
SHELBY PARK   18" x 24" Limited Edition Print created in 2011 by Andy Gregg
HADLEY PARK   18" x 24" Limited Edition Print created in 2011 by Edward Patton
NASHVILLE GREENWAYS   18" x 24" Limited Edition Print created in 2011 by Andy Gregg & Joel Anderson
PARTHENON   18" x 24" Limited Edition Print created in 2004 and updated in 2011 by Joel Anderson

PERCY PRIEST LAKE 18" x 24" Limited Edition Print created in 2006 by Joel Anderson

"The Spirit of Nashville Collection needed a manly print to counter the Ballet, Symphony, and Chamber Orchestra prints. So I chose a peaceful fishing scene in masculine tones as a way of celebrating Percy Priest Lake, Nashville's biggest playground for big boys and their toys."

RADNOR LAKE 18" x 24" Limited Edition Print created in 2005 by Joel Anderson

"I went to Radnor many times to take reference photos as I planned the design of this poster. I explored colorful autumn leaves, bright, flowering springtime, and lush green summer foliage. Since I couldn't decide which season I liked best, I made the poster into a nighttime scene."

PERCY WARNER PARK

A vintage postcard depicting the main entrance to Percy Warner Park.

PERCY WARNER PARK, along with Edwin Warner Park are collectively known as "The Warner Parks." These beautiful wooded parks are the largest municipally administered parks in Tennessee, containing 2,684 acres of forest and field, nine miles from downtown Nashville.

In 1927, Colonel Luke Lea and Mrs. Percie Warner Lea deeded the initial 868 acres of land to the city, and named the park after her father, Percy Warner. Today, the parks are composed of two different tracts of land—lush, wooded expanses of rolling hills and open fields separated by the thin corridor of Old Hickory Boulevard. A system of linked hiking trails was developed in the 1930s by the Works Progress Administration and enhanced in the 1970s by the Youth Conservation Corps and Nature Center staff.

Virtually unchanged since their establishment in 1927, the parks' thick, hardwood forests provide cool shade, open fields, and a habitat for wildlife.

Over 500,000 people visit the Parks annually to utilize picnic areas, scenic roadways and overlooks, 12 miles of hiking trails, an equestrian center and horse trails, cross-country running courses, golf courses, athletic fields, nature center, a model-airplane flying field, and 9 miles of mountain biking trails.

Since 1941, the Iroquois Steeplechase has been running continuously at Percy Warner Park on the beautiful race course inspired by Marcellus Frost and designed by William DuPont. The widely renowned event has created a festive sporting spectacle that has become a rite of spring for Nashvillians. The National Steeplechase Association sanctions 41 race meets throughout the Eastern U.S., with Nashville hosting one of the finest race courses. The Iroquois Steeplechase brings more than 25,000 people into Percy Warner Park each year to enjoy the all-day event while raising funds for charity.

< PERCY WARNER PARK 18" x 24" Limited Edition Print created in 2005 by Kristi Carter Smith

"I wanted to do a loose, impressionistic poster to add some texture to the Spirit of Nashville Collection. Middle Tennessee foliage can be spectacular, and I wanted to hint at the pleasure of the sights and smells of this beautiful park on a sunny autumn day."

EDWIN & PERCY WARNER PARKS 18" x 24" Limited Edition Print created in 2012 by Michael Korfhage & Joel Anderson

"It is not uncommon for hikers to hear the hoot of an owl while exploring the shady wooded trails in Percy Warner Park."

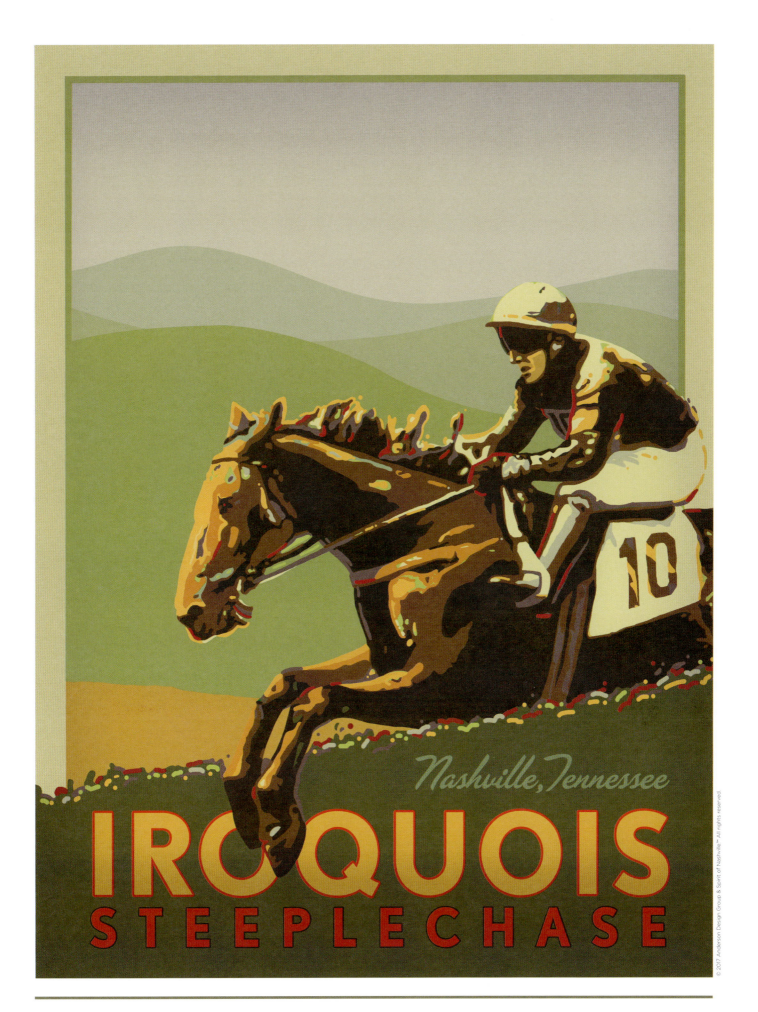

IROQUOIS STEEPLECHASE   18" x 24" Limited Edition Print created in 2003 by Joel Anderson

"The pomp and spectacle of this annual event would be hard to depict in a single poster design. So I opted to focus on the horse race rather than the social aspect of this high society gala. To capture the energy of the event, I created a bold image of a horse and rider bursting over a hedge."

PUBLIC SQUARE PARK

NASHVILLE'S CIVIC HEART SINCE 1784.

METRO PARKS NASHVILLE

COURT HOUSE

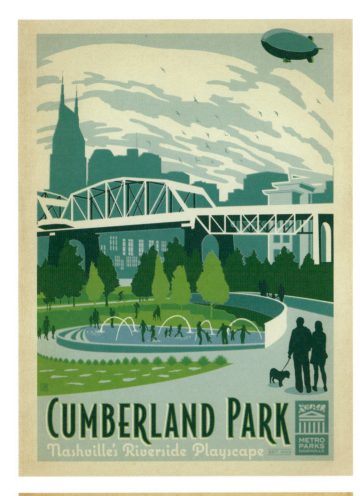

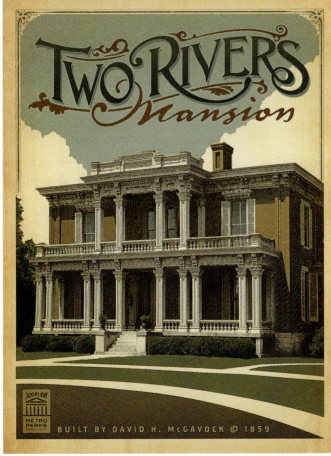

< PUBLIC SQUARE PARK   18" x 24" Limited Edition Print created in 2012 by Andy Gregg
CUMBERLAND PARK   18" x 24" Limited Edition Print created in 2012 by Michael Korfhage & Joel Anderson
BELLS BEND PARK   18" x 24" Limited Edition Print created in 2012 by Ligia Teodosiu
TWO RIVERS MANSION   18" x 24" Limited Edition Print created in 2011 by Joel Anderson
FANNIE MAE DEES PARK (DRAGON PARK)   18" x 24" Limited Edition Print created in 2012 by Andy Gregg

LOVELESS CAFE

Even after extensive renovations, the front of the Loveless Cafe looks almost exactly as it always did.

IF A NEWCOMER to Nashville asks where to get the best biscuits, the response is unanimous: the Loveless Cafe. Most locals know it's one of the best places for country ham, fresh preserves and their famous, made-from-scratch biscuits in a down-home atmosphere.

The roadhouse, with hardwood floors and red-and-white checkerboard cloths on the tables, isn't much different now than when Lon and Annie Loveless bought the property in 1951. At first, the Loveless Motel and Cafe was more of an outdoor venue, so to speak. The couple set up picnic tables outside and sold fried chicken and biscuits to hungry Natchez Trace travelers. As business grew, the Loveless' converted the rooms of the early 1900s home on the property into a dining room and kitchen. Lon smoked the hams, and Annie used her secret recipe to make perfect homemade biscuits, which she cut from the dough with a Campbell's Soup can.

Due to a decline in Lon's health, the Loveless' sold the motel and cafe to Cordell and Stella Maynard. The Maynards stayed true to the motel and cafe's original vibe; Annie even shared

the biscuit recipe so the restaurant could maintain its most authentic asset. After 14 years, the Maynards sold the business to Donna and Charles McCabe in 1973. Their 12-year-old son, George, helped do chores around the motel, and when he was old enough, became a partner in the business in 1982.

George expanded the business by offering the Hams & Jams mail order catalog, allowing customers to ship the country goodness anywhere in the world. The McCabes focused more on the new mail-order business, and shut down the motel portion of the business in 1985.

Part of the reason for the wait was the restaurant's ever-growing popularity. Personalities such as Willard Scott and George Jones have feasted on ham and grits. Superstar Paul McCartney had a bite to eat with Chet Atkins when he stopped by—and he even sang "Happy Birthday" to a fellow customer who was celebrating her 16th birthday.

The restaurant has received nods from *USA Today*, *Southern Living*, and even Martha Stewart herself. By 2003, the nearly century old-home could no longer keep up with the demands that the Loveless had created. Nashville caterer Tom Morales and investors bought the Loveless in 2003, and made expansions and renovations. It reopened in 2004, and on that first day, a diner told a reporter, "it's as good as it ever was."

In 2009, the Loveless Barn was built, providing a 4,800 square-foot live music and event venue. Today, the Loveless serves more than 450,000 guests per year.

< LOVELESS CAFE 18" x 24" Limited Edition Print created in 2003 by Joel Anderson

"When we began listing landmarks to feature in the first series of Spirit of Nashville prints, the Loveless Cafe was at the top of our list. Loveless is best known for its biscuits and for the big blue neon-lit sign out front. So to capture the feeling of stepping back in time, we chose to depict an old Buick in front of the famous sign. I couldn't figure out how to get biscuits into the picture, but then, just seeing the sign brings to mind the taste and aroma of hot, steamy biscuits and country cooking!"

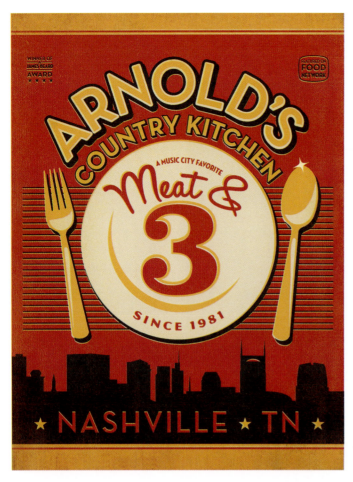

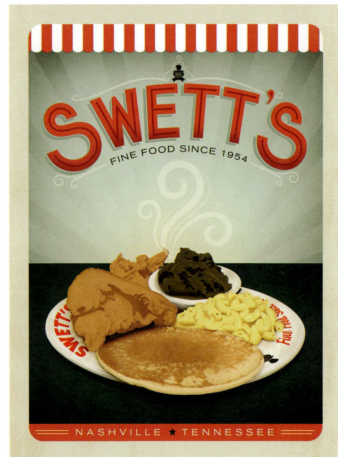
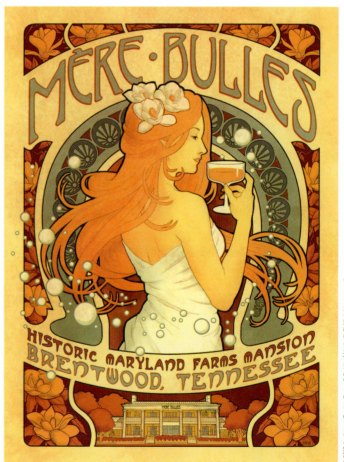

ARNOLD'S COUNTRY KITCHEN   18" x 24" Limited Edition Print created in 2012 by Joel Anderson
BOBBIE'S DAIRY DIP   18" x 24" Limited Edition Print created in 2012 by Andy Gregg
SWETT'S   18" x 24" Limited Edition Print created in 2012 by Edward Patton
MÈRE BULLES   18" x 24" Limited Edition Print created in 2013 by Aaron Johnson

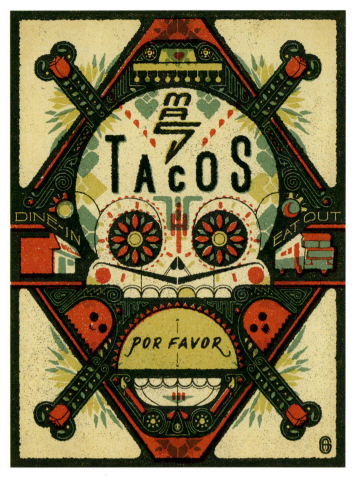
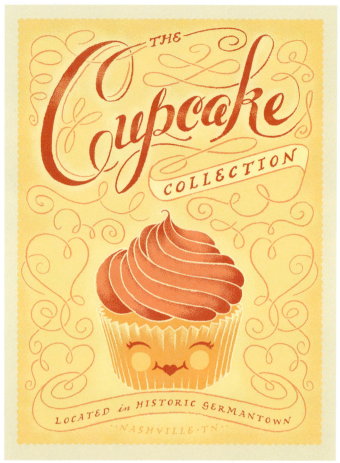

MAS TACOS POR FAVOR   18" x 24" Limited Edition Print created in 2012 by Andy Gregg
THE CUPCAKE COLLECTION   18" x 24" Limited Edition Print created in 2012 by Ligia Teodosiu
FIDO   18" x 24" Limited Edition Print created in 2012 by Ligia Teodosiu
THE PEANUT SHOP   18" x 24" Limited Edition Print created in 2012 by Joel Anderson

FARMERS' MARKET

Scenes of fresh fruits and vegetables from inside the Nashville Farmers' Market, located on 8th Avenue near the State Capitol.

Photos by Joel Anderson; Logo by Anderson Design Group

JUST AS THE DAY BEGINS to heat up, people from all over Middle Tennessee begin to make their way down aisles lined with barrels of fresh greens, red onions and vine-ripened tomatoes.

Some know exactly what they're looking for, but others just come to the Nashville Farmers' Market to stroll from stall to stall, seeing if they can find some locally grown treasure such as pole beans, blackberries, or a flat of budding flowers.

But more than just a place to buy produce, the market has served as one of Nashville's gathering places for more than 50 years; people stop and chat with familiar faces, or come just to buy from that local grower they now consider a friend. Often the person who's selling to you is a second or third-generation farmer, having spent a majority of their childhood helping out at the Farmers' Market.

People now visit the market on 8th Avenue North, but before it was built in the early 1950s, local farmers set up shop around the courthouse. Traffic became such a problem that the state legislature approved a bond issue in 1949 to build a permanent structure.

In 1993, the market received a face-lift; the building's extension from Jefferson Street back to Harrison Street would add five acres, providing space for additional, roomier stalls, groceries and restaurants. The new facility would be marketed as a part of the state's Bicentennial Mall project, scheduled for completion in 1996.

With the new space came even more diversity. Now alongside fresh vegetables, visitors could shop for ethnic meats, coffee, hot sauce, African and Jamaican products. Or they could try a gyro, homemade fudge or stir-fry at one of the many eateries.

In 2010, the Farmers' Market suffered severe damage during the May Flood. Thanks to the efforts of many kind folks, the market has been restored with expanded offerings such as classes, festivals and chef demonstrations. The important things still remain: it is a great place to find great food and a diverse community.

< FARMERS' MARKET   18" x 24" Limited Edition Print created in 2003 by Kristi Carter Smith

"We were going for a classic, earthy feel for this poster—one that might have been seen in an old feed store from the 1940s. The marketing team for the Nashville Farmers' Market liked our art so much they hired our studio to create a new logo, sign and web site with a similar feel to this print. The Farmers' Market is very eclectic place, so a basket of tomatoes doesn't quite tell the whole story. We may end up doing a series of posters to celebrate the wide variety of flowers, locally grown produce and international groceries this wonderful place has to offer."

PURITY DAIRIES

IN 1981, MILES EZELL, SR. wrote these words to his children: "Share your earthly goods as well as your time and talent with the Lord and others who are in need of it…Work hard, make money and spend wisely. Don't try to keep up with the Joneses. Continue to have a humble spirit as you now have. Be truthful and honest."

Left: Men drinking milk in front of a 50s era delivery truck. Right: Purity Founder Miles Ezell.

It's these tenets and others that are at the heart of Purity Dairies, an 81-year-old, Nashville-born-and-raised business. Since the late 20s, the Ezell family has strived to produce the best dairy products, and use what they've been given to reach out to the community.

In 1926, Miles and Estelle Ezell were newlyweds, and they lived with his parents on a small dairy farm owned by Dr. C.N. Cowden. Dr. Cowden wanted to return to practicing medicine full time, and approached Miles about buying the dairy. Knowing he had no money, Dr. Cowden agreed to rent him 60 cows, an old delivery truck and equipment for $450 a month, and helped him secure a loan for the first month's expenses. With those items in place, Ezell's Dairy was born.

A year later, Ezell rented a 200-acre farm on Edmondson Pike and bought several new cows on credit, as Dr. Cowden had to sell his cows. He traded in his 1923 Ford Coupe for a delivery truck, and Ezell's Dairy was standing on its own. Although the dairy was at the bottom of the Nashville dairy totem pole, Miles worked tirelessly to gain business and produce a quality product. His strong reputation helped him grow through the Great Depression, and by 1945, the first section of the Murfreesboro Road operation was built. The following year, Ezell merged with Rosebank Dairies, and the coupling took on a new name: Purity.

Over the years, Purity would be at the forefront of the dairy industry, introducing refrigerated delivery trucks, non-wax milk cartons and a recognizable advertising campaign. The dairy also bought out some of its biggest competitors: Richmond Pure Milk Company, Swiss Dairy Farm, and Murfreesboro Pure Milk Company. Generations of Ezells have been involved with the family business; although Dean Foods bought Purity in 1998, it's still a family business—Miles' grandson, Mark Ezell, serves as CEO.

And while delivering superior dairy products has always been paramount, the moral responsibility of giving back what's so richly been given to them is equally important. The Golden Rule has always been at the heart of the Purity philosophy. As Miles once said, "I just tried to produce milk that I would've drunk myself. I tried not to sell anything I didn't want my family to use. That went along with treating people as I wanted to be treated."

"What is black and white, has horns and gives great milk? A Purity home delivery truck!" The dairy's first milk truck (above) and a modern day truck (below).

All photos courtesy of Purity Dairies

< PURITY DAIRIES 18" x 24" Limited Edition Print created in 2003 by Joel Anderson

"This print was based on a photo taken by one of Nashville's top photographers, Dean Dixon. We worked with Dean to create imagery for a line of novelty ice cream products for Purity Dairies. After designing the packaging, the original photos sat unused for several years. When we decided to celebrate Purity Dairies as one of Nashville's great traditions, this Norman Rockwell-esque scene was the clear favorite for the poster image."

VANDYLAND

Mack McGee, owner Mitch Givens, Councilman George Armistead, and Elien Prisher celebrate Vandyland's 60th Anniversary.

It was a sad day when Vandyland closed its doors in May, 2006 and the familiar sign — a West End landmark — was removed from the storefront.

FOR MORE THAN SEVEN decades, Vandyland, and its predecessor, Candyland, was a Nashville landmark, especially for those with a sweet tooth. Kids hoped that a long afternoon downtown may be rewarded with a gourmet sweet treat from Candyland. And those who frequented the downtown location knew that they'd be greeted with a smile from Mack McGee and their "usual", made by one of the beloved staffers, before they could even sit down.

Over time, Vandyland became more than just a place to get a hot meal or a cool milkshake; it was a gathering place for young and old. So while the restaurant closed in 2006, many still hold fond memories of the restaurant on West End.

Vandyland's history actually starts with the opening of Candyland, at 817 Broadway, in the early 1900s. The shop later moved to its Church Street location and thrived there until its closing in 1986. Greek immigrant Billy Pappas, who was a cousin of one of the co-owners of the downtown location, opened the second Candyland location on West End in 1928; he became sole owner in 1945. Pappas died in 1985, and because of legalities, the new owner, Mitch Givens, had to change the name. The swap of one letter would reflect the culinary landmark's proximity to Vanderbilt University, thus calling it Vandyland.

Over the years, a who's who of Nashville (and beyond) strolled through Vandyland's doors. Former Tennessean publisher John Seigenthaler once worked there as a soda jerk. State Speaker of the House Jimmy Naifeh conducted business over chicken salad, and George W. Bush's campaign trail led there, maybe at the same time country star George Jones was sitting down for a bite to eat.

But no matter who you were, everyone was given the same special treatment. Longtime patron Glenda Higgins wrote: Vandyland was a "way of life" for many people—from regulars to those who moved and visited Vandyland upon each return to Nashville. The restaurant was a rendezvous for people from all walks of life. Myriads of special relationships evolved from the Candyland-Vandyland experience."

> "As soon as we heard Vandyland was closing for good, my husband and I decided to take our whole family to enjoy one last meal at our favorite hangout. That meal was magical. At one point, not a word was being spoken—the entire family was focused on slurping the last drops from the last Vandyland milkshakes we would ever have. Happy slurping kids with eyes closed in ecstasy, the way our puppy looks when she is intently chewing on a bone—that is how I'll always remember Vandyland." — *Joel Anderson*

< VANDYLAND 18" x 24" Limited Edition Print created in 2003 by Darren Welch

"The chocolate shakes made with Purity ice cream were always a Vandyland favorite. Most of the sandwiches on the menu were ordinary delights that you could make at home, but the milkshakes and hand-dipped candies made a trip to Vandyland special. For this print, we decided on a bold and simple milkshake, playing up the lettering style from the sign."

FOX'S DONUT DEN

THE 50s-STYLE SIGN stands out from the trendy new surroundings of the Green Hills shopping district. For more than 30 years, Donut Den has been a meeting place for businessmen, a study hall for area students, and a haven for any Nashvillian with a sweet tooth.

While getting his doctorate in biology at Vanderbilt, Norman Fox needed a way to make extra money. He'd come in contact with Oliver Harlow, the owner of a donut shop chain that was in its twilight years, and Fox became the beneficiary of Harlow's 50 years of business experience and a superior donut recipe. Fox found a spot on Granny White Pike, where Pizza Perfect now stands; Barbara, Fox's wife, said they should name their new donut shop Donut Den, since foxes live in dens.

Fox moved the business to Green Hills in 1977, and the sign from Harlow's Memphis store was moved to top the new location. The little man on the sign that had been a mascot for Harlow would now represent Donut Den.

Over the years, the shop has become a literal Green Hills landmark—people often give the Donut Den as a sign you've gone too far or haven't gone far enough down Hillsboro Pike. But it's also become somewhat of a tradition. Locals gather to talk about sports or current events, parents take their kids for a treat, and college students know they can get a job there. Most of Dr. Fox's longtime employees started when they were in school. Overnight cook Harold Graves started working there in 1973 when he was a freshman at Lipscomb. He still works there, and Dr. Fox says he's one of the best employees ever. Great donuts, long-term relationships and friendly service is what has made Fox's Donut Den a favorite Nashville tradition.

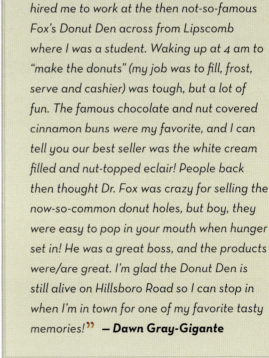

" *One of my favorite memories of growing up in Nashville was my first job. Norman Fox hired me to work at the then not-so-famous Fox's Donut Den across from Lipscomb where I was a student. Waking up at 4 am to "make the donuts" (my job was to fill, frost, serve and cashier) was tough, but a lot of fun. The famous chocolate and nut covered cinnamon buns were my favorite, and I can tell you our best seller was the white cream filled and nut-topped eclair! People back then thought Dr. Fox was crazy for selling the now-so-common donut holes, but boy, they were easy to pop in your mouth when hunger set in! He was a great boss, and the products were/are great. I'm glad the Donut Den is still alive on Hillsboro Road so I can stop in when I'm in town for one of my favorite tasty memories!* " — **Dawn Gray-Gigante**

< FOX'S DONUT DEN 18" x 24" Limited Edition Print created in 2006 by Joel Anderson

"It was just a matter of time before we selected the Donut Den to be in the Spirit of Nashville Collection. It's always been a favorite stop for my kids on those rare days when we have extra time before school starts. I've always loved the faded neon sign that adorns the old den of dietary iniquity. So when I started on the poster, it practically designed itself... that happy little Dutch boy with four fingers on one hand and no fingers on the other was destined to be the poster child for Nashville's favorite fresh baked delights!"

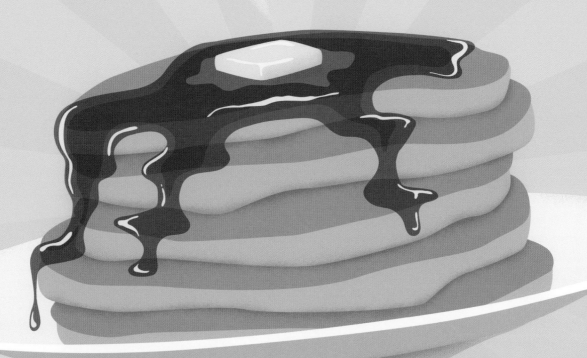

PANCAKE PANTRY

Scenes from the early days at the Pancake Pantry shot in August 1961—not much has changed, besides the hair styles!

IT'S NOT UNCOMMON, especially on a Saturday morning, to drive down 21st Avenue South, and see a line of people curving around the sidewalk and into the Pancake Pantry.

College students stand next to investment bankers, area residents line up behind Vanderbilt professors—you may even see a few locally-based country music stars or the occasional Tennessee Titan patiently waiting to dig into some light, fluffy pancakes or omelet filled with sausage or ham.

But no matter who they are, they'll say the same thing: it's worth the wait.

Bob Baldwin opened the pancake eatery in 1961. A Cornell University graduate, Baldwin was a traveling Hotpoint-appliance salesman when he met Jim Gerding, owner of the Pancake Pantry in Gatlinburg, TN. When he saw the Gatlinburg restaurant, Baldwin thought the concept would do well in Nashville. Baldwin opened the Hillsboro Village location, and it's been a local favorite since.

Two years after opening, Joyce Stubblefield was hired as a waitress. It wouldn't take long for her to become just as much of an institution as the restaurant itself. The customers know her, and she knows her customers. If you came there often, she may just bring you your "usual." When she celebrated her 30th anniversary in 1993, country superstars Kathy Mattea and Pam Tillis sent flowers. She was like a mother to a lot of stars up and down Music Row.

But the real star here is the pancakes. Serving more than 20 kinds, owner David Baldwin (Bob Baldwin's son) makes sure the light, fluffy pancakes with the rich, warm syrups bring people through those doors just like they did in 1961. Those who frequent the restaurant say they love the sweet potato pancakes with cinnamon cream syrup, and the famous buttermilk pancakes with the maple syrup can't be beat.

But it's the combination of good service and great food that keeps people coming back to this Nashville landmark. As owner David Baldwin says, "We stopped selling pancakes years ago; now we're in the business of building relationships."

"Fan art" from some young pancake eaters. Favorite artwork is featured on the frequently updated children's menus.

<PANCAKE PANTRY   18" x 24" Limited Edition Print created in 2004 by Emily Keafer

"I LOVE eating at the Pancake Pantry. The sweet potato pancakes with cinnamon cream syrup are my absolute favorite, but I chose to go with the traditional (yet still tasty!) buttermilk pancakes for this design. Nothing says 'Good Morning!' like a tower of fluffy flap jacks drizzled with gooey syrup and held aloft in front of a sunny yellow sky."

ELLISTON PLACE SODA SHOP

A JUKEBOX on every table—you don't see that anymore! Although Elliston Place has changed time and time again over the years, the Elliston Place Soda Shop remains. It may have changed ownership, but the tile floors, old-fashioned soda fountain, and good ole country meat-and-threes still remain.

The soda shop was actually the offspring of a pharmacy, which was in that location on Elliston Place when the street was largely residential. Dan Sanders owned the Elliston Place Pharmacy at 2113 Church Street, and by the late 1920s, he also owned the retail space next door. It's said that Doc Sanders was known for his storytelling abilities, and customers loved that he had fountain service, curb service and home delivery, which was usually made by bicycle.

In 1939, Lynn Chandler, 23, was offered the pharmacy's luncheonette business. (Chandler had practically grown up in a pharmacy, working at Noble's Pharmacy at age 9.) He used $234 of the $250 he'd saved to buy food and supplies. It was reported that, in those early days, Chandler would stick around outside the business after it was closed, hoping someone would come by wanting to buy something. If they did he'd reopen just for them, and sit and chat with them.

"You have to make a friend before you can make a customer," Chandler once said in a newspaper article.

Over the years, people, both famous and not so famous, sat on the stools at the Elliston Place Soda Shop and ordered thick, creamy milkshakes or a hot plate full of fried chicken or turkey and dressing. In 1989, the restaurant turned 50. In 1996, Eleanor Clay bought the soda shop from the Chandlers, and would later buy their trio of Sylvan Park Restaurants. After a brief ownership by Charles Galbreath from 1998 to 2003, Clay bought Elliston Place Soda Shop back.

In 2011, Elliston Place Soda Shop nearly closed down when it was time for the lease to be renegotiated. Rough economic times, plus an increase in the rent made it look like the old Nashville icon would not continue to survive. A public outpouring of support caused the landlord to restructure the lease so that Music City would not lose another cherished link to the past.

Today after more than 70 years, customers can still count on the same great food, sweet treats, and steady service that was there when Doc Sanders was still behind the pharmacy counter.

< ELLISTON PLACE SODA SHOP 18" x 24" Limited Edition Print created in 2005 by Aruna Rangarajan and Joel Anderson
"This print shows off the famous neon sign in front of the soda shop. We had to take some artistic license to get the Nashville skyline in the background, since the skyline is actually obstructed by the colossal buildings of the Baptist Hospital complex (now called St. Thomas Midtown.)"

BONGO JAVA

IT'S HIP, COOL, eclectic, and has always been way ahead of its time.

Before Starbucks was a household name in Nashville, there was Bongo Java, Nashville's oldest and most celebrated coffeehouse. The cafe opened March 28, 1993, and became world famous in December 1996 for the discovery of a cinnamon bun which many believe looks remarkably like Mother Teresa.

The bun was actually discovered on October 15, 1996 when store manager Ryan Finney was about to eat breakfast before the store opened. Something made Ryan look at the pastry he held in his hand before he ate it. He waited until the next employee came in, pushed the bun in front of his face and said, "What does this look like?" A barely awake and very surprised Todd Truly replied "Mother Teresa." The same test on the first few customers who came in that day confirmed the "miracle."

The NunBun™ was featured on the front page of The Tennessean the Saturday before Christmas. As a result, the story of the bun went world wide almost instantly, eventually reaching Calcutta, India. Bongo Java received a letter from Mother Teresa saying she didn't mind the bun itself but she didn't want them making money off of her name or image. The letter served to further the NunBun™'s fame. It was featured by media outlets around the world including The Washington Post, CNN, BBC, Paul Harvey's Radio Show, and The Late Show With David Letterman, making Bongo Java one of the most famous coffeehouses on the globe.

The story went quiet until 2005, when thieves broke into Bongo Java on Christmas Day and stole the famous Immaculate Confection. But even without the famous bun, Bongo Java continues to be a gathering place for all of Nashville, attracting musicians, students, artists and even some "employed" people as well!

> "From the gray wooden planks that line its front porch, to the whir of espresso machines and colorful baristas manning the counter, no place sets a mood of cool faster than Bongo Java. So for a permy-headed, department-store-clothes-wearing, fresh-faced freshman, no place could have been more intimidating. I admired Bongo Java from afar for several months before I ventured inside its walls. It wasn't until a national media frenzy erupted over the discovery of [the NunBun™] that my curiosity overcame me. I had to see [it]. I wasn't the only one, of course. Reporters, curious locals and college students waded past the patient "regulars"... to see the bun. As I stood in line wondering what on earth I'd order off the menu..., I spotted her. There she was—displayed under Plexiglas,... glorious in all her confectionary goodness. I had seen her, and my curiosity had been satisfied. More importantly, I had made it inside the über-hip Bongo Java. I knew I [now] had a place to come when I needed a break, some study time or space to reflect. Bongo Java was hip, but it was also warm and welcoming. I looked around and saw businessmen drinking their java next to bohemian types, college students polishing up papers next to politicians strategizing their next move. Under the watchful eye of the NunBun™, I realized that all walks of life were welcomed at Bongo. And I imagined that's just the way Mother Teresa would have it." — **Cara Davis**

< BONGO JAVA 18" x 24" Limited Edition Print created in 2003 by Matt Lehman

"Most people think that designers just sit around wearing black turtlenecks drinking coffee while slouching in front of a Mac laptop. So what's wrong with that? You can't create a poster like this drinking iced tea, wearing a seersucker suit!"

HOG HEAVEN

NASHVILLE is a great place for eating high on the hog. And if you are lucky enough to make it to Hog Heaven, you'll never want to come back down to earth! Even though the tiny shack is tucked away on a little side street next to a giant city park, this BBQ joint is a bona fide Nashville landmark. With outdoor seating for 3,000 (the front porch faces the sprawling lawns of Centennial Park), Hog Heaven features some of the best BBQ in town—and all within view of the Parthenon.

Located at 115 27th Ave North, this little slice of Heaven serves up what many swear is the best hand-pulled pork, chicken, beef and breast of turkey BBQ not only in Nashville, but on the planet. Owners Andy and Katy Garner bought the restaurant in 1989, after it had already been in business for 3 years. "We've always worked in the restaurant business and we wanted to run our own place. When we sampled the turkey sandwich and white sauce, we were in Hog Heaven—and we knew

Co-owner Katy Garner stands in the gates of heaven.

without a doubt that this was a concept to build on" says Katy. Since they bought the place, they've added beef brisket, chicken, and improved on a few of the recipes.

Hog Heaven has been featured on Food Network, Turner Network's *Blue Ribbon* show, Yahoo's *In Search of Real Food*, and voted Best BBQ by Nashville City Search several times over the years.

It may not be much to look at, but Hog Heaven is the real deal. But don't take our word for it; here is what some satisfied Hog Heaven fans have to say:

"I can definitely see why they call this Hog Heaven rather than Hog Purgatory."
—Wendy Williams

"The White Sauce isn't just a sauce, it's a way of life." —Cate Nance

"The building is small, the sandwiches are big, and Andy and Katy are about 5'9."
—Dayna Shaw

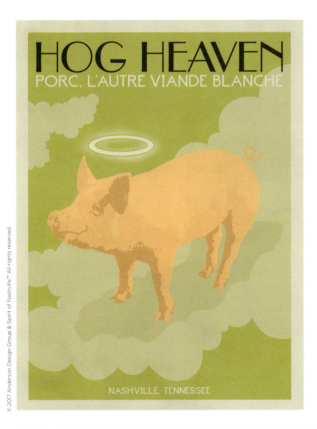

Food Network discovered the locally-famous BBQ Fight Club sauces and came to do a feature on Hog Heaven. Then the sauces started selling nationwide. We designed the Hog Heaven logo, sign, menu and label art in trade for 3 years worth of free BBQ. It was a great ride!

< This is the first Hog Heaven poster we created in 2003 as a part of the initial Spirit of Nashville print series. The art was created by Darren Welch.

< HOG HEAVEN BBQ FIGHT CLUB (PUNCHIN' PIG)   18" x 24" Limited Edition Print created in 2012 by Andy Gregg

"The food is amazing even if the restaurant looks like a summer campground cafeteria. As much as we love this dive, we just could not make a nice piece of art that featured a picture of the actual restaurant. So we ended up doing a poster to promote their amazing BBQ Fight Club sauces."

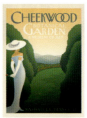

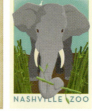
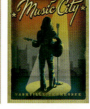

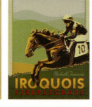

About the Art and the Artists...

THE SPIRIT OF NASHVILLE print collection came together as I was thinking of a way to showcase Nashville to my out-of-town clients and friends. At first, it was a publicity stunt to convince clients from New York or L.A. that Nashville was a hip place with a lot to offer. (Back then, folks didn't realize how cool it is to be Southern!) As founder of Anderson Design Group, I was looking for a way to show off our firm's illustration and design skills while shining a spotlight on Music City's most interesting, delicious and unique features.

I joined forces with McQuiddy Printing, formerly one of Nashville's oldest printers, to create a giant 18" x 30" limited edition calendar that would feature 14 illustrated prints of my favorite Nashville landmarks, restaurants, and cultural icons. I asked my creative team to join me in the massive challenge of rendering all of these designs in the tradition of the Golden Age of Poster Art, a glorious period of hand-illustrated and hand-lettered poster art which spanned from the late 1800s to the mid-1900s. After hundreds of hours of research, reference photography, drawing, painting, and designing, we finished the calendar and produced 1,500 copies. The rest is history. We ran out of calendars in just a few weeks. People were calling from as far away as Canada asking where they could buy the prints they had seen. We soon realized we had stumbled onto something big. People were cutting up our calendars and framing the art!

The prints from the 2004 calendar won numerous design and illustration awards, and the requests for prints began to increase to the point that we started thinking about ways to make the art available to the public.

In 2005, the Spirit of Nashville Collection was officially born when we decided to create another set of designs that would not only be bound into a promotional wall calendar, but would also be produced as a limited edition run of ready-to-frame prints. The Metro Arts commission selected the entire print series for exhibition in the Nashville International Airport. Soon, the Spirit of Nashville Collection was doing more than promoting our design firm—it also was proving to be a great promotional tool for the city and the establishments depicted in the art. We began looking for nonprofit organizations who could benefit from some extra exposure, and we created posters for notable establishments such as the Nashville Zoo, Andrew Jackson's Hermitage, The Frist Center for the Visual Arts, and the Nashville Ballet. We were on a roll, and we kept adding new designs to the collection each year. Today, the Spirit of Nashville series includes over 150 different prints, celebrating our city's rich and diverse history, culture and enduring charm.

New lines of poster art sprang from the success of the Spirit of Nashville Collection. Poster art fans and collectors from other cities began to ask for designs featuring their home towns. I have always loved vintage travel posters. So I began creating new designs depicting contemporary landmarks, but rendered in a classic style similar to our Spirit of Nashville designs. The Art & Soul of America Collection was born as a new poster series celebrating

About the Art and the Artists...

our nation's favorite destinations. After creating more than 150 different prints of U.S. cities and national parks, I began creating new series like World Travel prints, the Coastal Collection, Coffee themes, Mid-Century Modern design, Music Festivals, Southern Expressions, Vintage Americana Advertising art, and a Man Cave collection. By 2016, Anderson Design Group had produced over 800 different poster designs. Our art has been exhibited on every continent on the globe (except for Antarctica.) Our prints have been purchased for display all over Europe, Australia, South Africa, Canada, and South America. They have been featured on movie and network TV sets, given as gifts to diplomats, hung in embassies and consulates, published in design journals, and displayed in homes and offices by poster art lovers everywhere. What started in Nashville as a way to celebrate Music City and promote our little Nashville-based design firm has grown to become one of the largest bodies of decorative poster art ever assembled by one team of artists. While we have slowed down on Nashville art, we are still creating new art for other cities.

As we proceed, we continue to abide by the belief that good poster art is all about strong, simple, beautiful composition. Poster art says hello to your brain, and then strikes up a long-term relationship with your heart. Effective poster design is meant to catch your eye from a distance, and then speak to your soul upon closer inspection. It is created to be affordable and accessible—simple enough to be enjoyed by anyone, yet profound enough to move everyone.

Every artist on my team, including my-

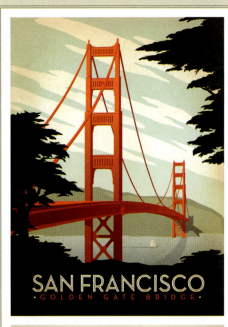  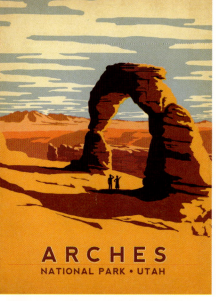

Shown above are prints from the Art & Soul of America series, the Coastal Collection, the World Travel series, and Southern Delights.

self, never stops learning and developing, honing skills, and being inspired by great artists of the early 20th Century. Even after creating poster art for over 30 years, I am still amazed at the beautiful things yesterday's artists cranked out in an era before photography was widely used in advertising art. They would paint and draw, creating temporary art that was produced to be pasted onto a wall to catch someone's attention as they hurried past. Their every-day advertising art had to be bold, iconic, emotive, and easily read in a split second. And it was done by very talented artists who never dreamed that their work would be collected and prized by future generations like ours.

We use the computer as a finishing tool, but I still insist that my artists draw and sketch to create art that is as authentic and iconic as the classic 20th Century works that inspire us. There is no quick or simple way to do this kind of art. Just like in the old days, each poster starts with a clever idea, and takes 30 to 60 hours to render. Years ago, poster art was disposable, (that is why the few surviving vintage posters are so rare and valuable today). And that is why we are creating a new generation of poster art which hopefully will not suffer the same fate of being pasted up on a wall, only to fade in the sun, peel in the wind, and disintegrate in the rain!

As you've seen in this book, everything we do is a labor of love, rooted in our appreciation of classic American advertising art. Check out more of our design work and poster art in the Anderson Design Group Studio Store located at 116 29th Ave. North, Nashville, TN, or online at www.ADGstore.com. — *Joel Anderson*

  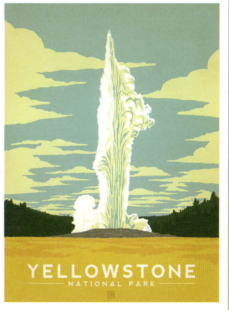
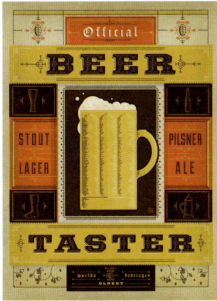  

Shown above are more prints from the Art & Soul of America series, the Mod Collection, the Man Cave series, and the Coffee Collection.

INFORMATION SOURCES

These stories were written by Angela Patterson. Her research sources are listed below:

Belle Meade Plantation Sources:
www.bellemeadeplantation.com
www.bonps.org

Belmont University Sources:
Belmont Mansion Web site (www.belmontmansion.com/home.htm)
Belmont University Web site (www.belmont.edu/umac/belmont_history/250_word_history.html)
Davis, L. (1948, December 5). Woman-Run Belmont. The Nashville Tennessean Magazine.
Davis, L. (1986, October 26). Two faces of Belmont look on campus, city. The Tennessean.
Kreyling, C., Paine, W., Warterfield, C.W., and Wiltshire, S.F. (Eds.) (1996). Classical Nashville: Athens of the South. Nashville: Vanderbilt University Press.
The Tennessee Encyclopedia for History and Culture Web site (tennesseeencyclopedia.net/--entries for Adelicia Acklen, Belmont College, Ward-Belmont and Belmont University)

Bicentennial Mall Source:
Hinton, K. G., (1997). A Long Path: The Search for a Tennessee Bicentennial Landmark. Hillsboro Press: Franklin, TN.

Bluebird Cafe Sources:
A. Kurland, personal communication, May 16, 2007.
Bluebird Cafe Web site (www.bluebirdcafe.com/about/history.htm)

Chaffin's Barn Sources:
Adkins, Tim. (2002, May). Dinner with a show. The Tennessean.
Chaffin's Barn Dinner Theatre Web site (www.dinnertheatre.com/welcome.html)
Personal correspondence, Janie Chaffin, June 2007.

Cheekwood Sources:
Tennessee Encyclopedia of History and Culture Web site (tennesseeencyclopedia.net/)
Written history provided by Cheekwood Museum of Art

Donut Den Sources:
Blackwood, Suzanne Normand. (2004, March 25). Donut Den: A delectable treat for many. The Tennessean.
Fox, N. Personal Communication, May 30, 2007.

Elliston Place Soda Shop Sources:
Beasley, K. (1991, March 20). Soda Shop Shakes for 52 Years. Nashville Banner.
Carey, B. (1996, May 22). Soda Shop Sold, but Historic Charm to Remain. Nashville Banner.
Chappell, S. (1989, September 16). Soda Shop a Landmark on Elliston. Nashville Banner.
Deville, N. (2003, August 19). Former Owner Back at Helm of Elliston Place Soda Shop. The Tennessean.

Fisk University Sources:
The Fisk University Web site (www.fisk.edu/page.asp?id=115)
The Fisk Jubilee Singers Web site (www.fiskjubileesingers.org/our_history.html)
The Tennessee Encyclopedia of History and Culture Web site (tennesseeencyclopedia.net/imagegallery.php?EntryID=F020)

Frist Center for the Visual Arts Sources:
Traditional Fine Arts Organization Web site (www.tfaoi.com/aa/4aa/4aa410.htm)
Frist Center for the Visual Arts Web site (www.fristcenter.org/site/about/)

General Jackson Showboat Sources:
Battle, Bob. (1983, December 20). Opryland's showboat plan steaming full speed ahead. Nashville Banner.
Battle, Bob. (1984, October 10). Showboat to offer four trips daily. Nashville Banner.
Battle, Bob. (1985, March 27.) Opryland showboat taking to water. Nashville Banner.
Canfield, Clarke. (1985, June 24). The showboat's finally come to town! Nashville Banner.
Gaylord Opryland Web site (www.gaylordhotels.com/gaylordopryland/meetings/gjack/)

Hatch Show Print Sources:
Hance, M. (1991, December 10). History packs up, moves to Broadway. Nashville Banner.
Hatch Show Print pages on the Country Music Hall of Fame Web site (www.countrymusichalloffame.com/site/experience-hatch-history.aspx)
Sherraden, J., Horvath, E. and Kingsbury, P. (2001). Hatch Show Print: The History of a Great American Poster Shop. San Francisco: Chronicle Books.
York, M. (1982, October 31). Old-Time Print Shop Values Early Style. The Tennessean.

The Hermitage and The War of 1812 Source:
www.thehermitage.com

Lipscomb University Sources:
David Lipscomb Campus School Web Site (dlcs.lipscomb.edu/page.asp?SID=85&Page=2561)
Lipscomb University Web site (www.lipscomb.edu/content.asp?SID=4&CID=2117)
Hooper, Robert. (1977). David Lipscomb: More Than an Editor. Retrieved from (www.gospeladvocate.com/lipscomb.htm).
Tennessee Encyclopedia of History and Culture Web Site (tennesseeencyclopedia.net)

Loveless Cafe Sources:
19 Things You Didn't Know About....The Loveless Cafe. (2002, May 5). The Tennessean.
Ghianni, T. (1992, August 13). Long live beloved Loveless. Nashville Banner.
Lawson, R. (2003, November 27). Renovations to brighten future of Loveless. The Tennessean.
Loveless Cafe Web site (www.lovelesscafe.com/lovelesshistory.html)
Naujeck, J. A. (2006, June 29). Resurrected Loveless Cafe 'just as good as it ever was'. The Tennessean.

Montgomery Bell Academy Source:
Montgomery Bell Academy Web site

Nashville Ballet Source:
Davis, L. Personal Communication, May 10, 2007.

Nashville Farmers' Market Sources:
Duke, M. and Gerlock, K. (1993, April 19). Design would add 5 acres to market. Nashville Banner.
Goad, K. (1993, August 12). Farmers' Market planners site 21st century. Nashville Banner.
Kerr, G. (1995, July 24). Market Promises an Ethnic Extravaganza. The Tennessean.
Nashville Farmers' Market Web site (www.nashvillefarmersmarket.org/history.html)
Williams, J. B. (1986, May). "Farmers' Market: Pick of the Crop." Nashville Magazine.

Nashville Shakespeare Festival Source:
Personal correspondence

Nashville Symphony Sources:
Nashville Symphony Web site (www.nashvillesymphony.org/main.taf?p=2,11)
Hinton, A. (2006, May 11). A true work in progress. The City Paper.
Simbeck, R. (1996). The Nashville Symphony Celebrates 50 Seasons. Nashville: Nashville Symphony.

Natchez Trace Bridge Sources:
Nova page—PBS Web site (www.pbs.org/wgbh/nova/bridge/meetarch.html)
PCL Civil Constructors Web site (www.pcl.com/projects/Archived/5500600/index.aspx)
The Tennessee Encyclopedia for History and Culture (tennesseeencyclopedia.net)

Pancake Pantry Sources:
Arnold, Bernie. (1989, May 31). Pancakes make breakfast flat-out best. Nashville Banner.
Ippolito, Mark. (1993, May 15). Stars stop by to congratulate 'Momma'. The Tennessean.
Keel, Pinckney. (1979, November 29). Second Home at the Pantry. The Tennessean.

The Parthenon Sources:
Kreyling, C., Paine, W., Warterfield, C.W., and Wiltshire, S.F. (Eds.) (1996). Classical Nashville: Athens of the South. Nashville: Vanderbilt University Press.
Nashville Parks and Recreation Web site (www.nashville.gov/Parthenon/History.htm)

Purity Dairies Sources:
Promotional materials courtesy of Purity Dairies
Dudlicek, James. "Nashville Stars." Dairy Field. April 2007. Pgs. 18-22.

Ryman Auditorium Sources:
Nashville Public Television Web Site (www.wnpt.net/ryman/timeline/index.html)
Ryman Auditorium Web Site (www.ryman.com/)
Van West, C. (1998). Ryman Auditorium. In the Tennessee Encyclopedia of History and Culture. Pp. 820-821. Nashville: Rutledge Hill Press.
Zimmerman, P C. (1998). Tennessee Music: Its People and Places. San Francisco: Miller Freeman Books.

Tennessee State Capitol Sources:
Dekle, C. B. (1966). Tennessee State Capitol. Tennessee Historical Quarterly. Vol. 25, No.3. Pgs. 3-28.
Gadski, Mary Ellen. (1988). The Tennessee State Capitol: An Architectural History. Tennessee Historical Quarterly. Vol. 47, No. 2. Pgs. 67- 91.

Union Station Sources:
The Tennessee Encyclopedia of History and Culture
The Wyndham Union Station Hotel Web site
Cooney, Deborah, ed. "Speaking of Union Station: An Oral History of a Nashville Landmark." Williams Printing Co., 1977.
Sherman, Joe. "A Thousand Voices: The Story of Nashville's Union Station." Nashville: Rutledge Hill Press. 1987.

Vanderbilt University Sources:
Doll, G. (1994 Summer). Tales of the Commodore: Cornelius Vanderbilt at 200. Vanderbilt Magazine.
www.vanderbilt.edu
Vanderbilt University Special Collections and University Archives Virtual Reading Room

Vandyland Sources:
Blackwood, S. N. (2006, March 15). Customers say farewell to Vandyland. The Tennessean.
Courtney, R. (2006, April 7). Vandyland may not be dead yet; a plan is afoot. The City Paper.
Higgins, G. (2007, May 11). Reflections on West End's Candyland-Vandyland. The Tennessean.
Lawson, R. and Wood, T.E. (2006, February 24). Vandyland, R.I.P. Nashville Post.
Zepp, George. (2003, October 29). Candyland stirs sweet memories for many. The Tennessean.

Zoo Sources:
Nashville Zoo Website (http://www.nashvillezoo.org/about & http://www.nashvillezoo.org/our-blog/posts/city-invests-in-nashville-zoo)